Dynamic Models of Oligopoly

FUNDAMENTALS OF PURE AND APPLIED ECONOMICS

EDITORS-IN-CHIEF

J LESOURNE, Conservatoire National des Arts et Métiers, Paris, France
H SONNENCHEIN, Princeton University, Princeton, New Jersey, USA

ADVISORY BOARD

K ARROW, Stanford University, Stanford, California, USA (Nobel Prizewinner for Economics)
W BAUMOL, Woodrow Wilson School, Princeton University, Princeton, New Jersey, USA
W A LEWIS, Woodrow Wilson School, Princeton University (Nobel Prizewinner for Economics)
S TSURU, 8-11-4 Akasaka, Minato-ku, Tokyo 107, Japan

ISSN: 0883–2366

Dynamic Models
of Oligopoly

Drew Fudenberg
University of California, Berkeley, USA

and

Jean Tirole
Massachusetts Institute of Technology, Cambridge, USA

A Volume in the Theory of the Firm and Industrial Organization Section
edited by
A. Jacquemin
Université Catholique de Louvain, Belgium

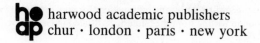 harwood academic publishers
chur · london · paris · new york

© 1986 by Harwood Academic Publishers GmbH, Poststrasse 22, 7000 Chur, Switzerland. All rights reserved.

Harwood Academic Publishers

P.O. Box 197
London WC2E 9PX
England

58, rue Lhomond
75005 Paris
France

P.O. Box 786
Cooper Station
New York, New York 10276
United States of America

Library of Congress Cataloging in Publication Data
Fudenberg, Drew.
    Dynamic models oligopoly.
    (Fundamentals of pure and applied economics,
ISSN 0883-2366; vol. 3. Theory of the firm and industrial organization section)
    Bibliography: p.
    Includes index.
    1. Oligopolies—Mathematical models. I. Tirole, Jean. II. Title. III. Series:
Fundamentals of pure and applied economics; v. 3. IV. Series: Fundamentals of pure and
applied economics. Theory of the firm and industrial organization section.
HD2757.3.F86   1986   338.8'2'0724   86-3142
ISBN 3-7186-0279-2

CONTENTS

INTRODUCTION TO THE SERIES

Drawing on a personal network, an economist can still relatively easily stay well informed in the narrow field in which he works, but to keep up with the development of economics as a whole is a much more formidable challenge. Economists are confronted with difficulties associated with the rapid development of their discipline. There is a risk of "balkanisation" in economics, which may not be favourable to its development.

Fundamentals of Pure and Applied Economics has been created to meet this problem. The discipline of economics has been subdivided into sections (listed on the inside back cover). These sections include short books, each surveying the state of the art in a given area.

Each book starts with the basic elements and goes as far as the most advanced results. Each should be useful to professors needing material for lectures, to graduate students looking for a global view of a particular subject, to professional economists wishing to keep up with the development of their science, and to researchers seeking convenient information on questions that incidentally appear in their work.

Each book is thus a presentation of the state of the art in a particular field rather than a step by step analysis of the development of the literature. Each is a high level presentation but accessible to anyone with a solid background in economics, whether engaged in business, government, international organizations, teaching, or research in related fields.

Three aspects of *Fundamentals of Pure and Applied Economics* should be emphasized:

—First, the project covers the whole field of economics, not only theoretical or mathematical economics.

—Second, the project is open-ended and the number of books is not predetermined. If new interesting areas appear, they will generate additional books.

—Last, all the books making up each section will later be grouped to constitute one or several volumes of an Encyclopaedia of Economics.

The editors of the sections are outstanding economists who have selected as authors for the series some of the finest specialists in the world.

J Lesourne   H Sonnenschein

Dynamic models of oligopoly†

DREW FUDENBERG and JEAN TIROLE

1. INTRODUCTION

THIS MONOGRAPH surveys some recent work on dynamic oligopoly. While we have tried to cover a selection of topics that is a
fairly representative sample of current research, these notes are
not intended as an exhaustive survey of the field. As will become
clear, we have to a large extent selected topics closely related to
our own work.

As the title suggests, we focus mainly on the formalization of
strategic relationships. We should acknowledge the literature
describing the behavior of a competitive firm as a dynamic control
problem (e.g., Gaskins [35], Jacquemin [47], Lesourne
[58]). This literature considered the dynamic problem of a firm
in a market environment that reacts in a specified exogenous way
to the firm's actions. While this approach was useful in developing
some preliminary intuition, it did not endogenize the firm's rivals'
reactions. This endogenization is precisely the object of the game-
theoretic models discussed in this monograph. Our methodological approach is complementary to the more thematic ones
which can be found in the industrial organization section of this
encyclopedia.

We have greatly benefited from the recent Kreps and Spence

†This survey is the outgrowth of lectures we gave at the Institute for
Mathematical Studies in the Social Sciences (IMSSS), Stanford University, in
the summer of 1983. Our research was supported by National Science Foun-
dation grants SES 81–04769 and SES 82–01373 at the IMSSS, and by SES
82–07925 at the University of California, Berkeley. The authors would like to
thank John Geanakoplos, David Kreps, Eric Maskin, John Roberts, Jose
Scheinkman and Robert Wilson for helpful conversations, and Mordecai Kurz
for encouraging us to undertake this project.

[54] survey, "Modelling the Role of History in Industrial Organization and Competition." Our work should be viewed as a complement to theirs: we cover a somewhat different set of models, and develop them in more detail. We have also geared our presentation to a more technically-minded audience.

Following Kreps and Spence, we can identify two reasons for employing dynamic models of oligopoly in preference to static ones. First, nonstationary industries, whether growing or declining, require explicitly dynamic models. Second, "of equal or perhaps greater importance is that the behavior and performance of a mature industry depend crucially on the history of that industry." We believe that this history-dependence is best modelled in explicitly dynamic models.

Let us begin with the second issue, that of the influence of history in mature industries. Even when the environment is stationary, dynamic considerations are still quite important.

The oldest and best-known approach to modelling history-dependence in oligopolies is supergame analysis. The basic idea, which goes back to Chamberlin [16], is that oligopolists realize their interdependence and thus do not choose outputs (or prices) under the assumption that their decision will have no effect on the actions of their competitors. Instead, they realize that a price cut may provoke retaliation, and thus have an incentive to behave more "cooperatively." Thus firms can attain a collusive payoff without the need for an explicit (contractual) agreement, because that payoff can be obtained in a noncooperative equilibrium. This is the game-theoretic explanation of "tacit collusion." As the supergame story is well known (see Friedman [27] for a detailed analysis, or Kreps and Spence, pp. 16–18, for a sketch), we will not work through it here. We will, however, discuss the recent work of Green and Porter [41] which extends the model to allow for random shocks in demand. In their model, a game-theoretic version of Stigler's [97] paper, firms cannot observe rivals' output but only the market price. This gives firms an extra incentive to cheat, because the resulting lower price may be blamed on the demand shock. We also discuss the paper by Brock and Scheinkman [12], on supergames with capacity constraints.

The problem with the supergame approach is that it is all too successful in producing tacit collusion. Supergames have lots of equilibria. While one might expect that the history of the industry would be the main determinant of which outcome would in fact occur, history has no direct role in supergame analysis, in the sense that given the strategies (which are common knowledge) each firm can compute its payoff to any sequence of choices. In supergames, the dependence of the equilibrium strategies on history is a sort of "bootstrap" phenomenon—each firm's strategy depends on the past only because the other firms' strategies do. Moreover, many different types of history-dependence are equilibria. The problem may be that supergame models are too abstract to predict oligopoly behavior. As Schelling [82] suggested, in moving from the detail of real games to the formalism of strategy spaces and payoffs, one may leave behind information that is crucial to predicting which equilibrium will occur. Schelling's theory of "focal points" emphasizes the importance of the names of the strategies ("twelve noon" is a focal point, 2:23 isn't) and cultural expectations (whether "left" or "right" is the focal point may depend on which side of the street one drives on) in determining behavior. Another, related, drawback of the supergame approach is that most games have a finite horizon. With a fixed finite horizon, backwards induction rules out the bootstrapping which supports most of the supergame equilibria. While supergame analysis easily extends to oligopolies in which there's a constant and small probability that each period is the last (so that the game does end with probability one), the set of equilibria is much closer to that with a fixed finite horizon if the final period is almost certain to be within a small band.

An alternative strategy for modelling tacit collusion and dynamic coordination is to incorporate directly into the model some reason for history to matter. The hope here is that including more of the "nitty-gritty" of oligopolistic competition may allow for more specific predictions. We will discuss two such alternative approaches—the work of Maskin and Tirole on short-run commitments, and the work of Kreps, Milgrom, Roberts and Wilson on games with incomplete information. Maskin and Tirole [63], [64] study oligopolies in which output (or price) is fixed in the very short run. Such markets are not totally static, because history matters, but the history-dependence is of the stationary variety which might be expected in a mature industry. Thus despite the commitments, the model fits under our second heading of the influence of history in mature industries.

In the incomplete information literature, the past matters, not because of a physical link between past and current variables, but rather because the past conveys information about some unknown characteristics of the other firms. This literature makes two methodological points. First, if the past is thought to matter because it signals future intentions, then the oligopoly model used can and should include uncertainty and inference. Second, incomplete information can explain how collusion can be an equilibrium outcome in repeated games with a *finite* horizon, by breaking the chain of backwards induction which, for example, yields "always cheat" as the only finite-horizon equilibrium of the repeated prisoner's dilemma.

We will call this form of incomplete-information model, which uses incomplete information to break a chain of backwards induction, one of "reputation effects." The distinguishing feature of a reputation-effects model is that while the *inference* procedure is clearly intended to be descriptive, the incomplete information itself need not be so interpreted. In the "reputation effects" models such as Kreps et al. [52], there is typically a very small amount of incomplete information, i.e., each player's unknown characteristic *almost certainly* has a particular, ("normal") value. This contrast with incomplete-information models such as Milgrom and Roberts [67] in which the incomplete information is itself descriptive, and nonnegligible probability is assigned to the various possible values of each player's characteristic. The distinction is one of emphasis. The "reputation-effects" models stress the difference that an epsilon of incomplete information can make. These papers may thus be viewed as testing the robustness of the associated complete-information model. Because the incompleteness of the information is small in reputation-effect models, it only matters if the game is repeated a number of times.[1]

---

1. In a recent survey, Wilson [100] uses "Reputation Effects" more broadly to include all signalling in games of incomplete information. We believe the distinction between "epsilon" and "very" incomplete information is useful, and have been able to think of no better name than "reputation effects" for the "epsilon-incomplete" case, although reputation is certainly an issue in, for example, the limit-pricing papers.

The reputation-effects approach to repeated games, at least in its existing incarnations, has had the virtue of making fairly specific predictions as to equilibrium outcomes. Thus this approach "permits one ... to 'explain' the equilibrium that arises as a consequence of the formally specified initial beliefs" (K-S). However, the "equilibrium that arises is extremely sensitive to the initial assessments" (beliefs). In fact, Fudenberg and Maskin [29] have recently shown that if one is willing to accept all types of incomplete information (in arbitrarily small amounts) then by varying the initial beliefs one can obtain any individually rational outcome as an equilibrium, so that in a formal sense we are back to the supergame case as far as predictions go. Of course, not all initial beliefs are equally plausible, so that the reputation-effects models can still be useful for choosing between equilibria. By recasting the problem as one of choosing between different beliefs, these models allow more information to be used in making predictions.

Next we come to the other broad group of dynamic models of oligopoly, those concerned with growing, immature industries, or more generally those concerned with explicitly non-stationary environments. The typical paper of this group identifies one particular "tangible" variable, such as the levels of the firms' capital stocks, defines (flow) payoffs for each level of that variable, and proceeds to analyze competition over that one variable in isolation. For example, if the variable in question were capacity, one specifies how the firms' profits in the product market at any point in time depend on the levels of the capital stocks. This approach thus assumes that the manner in which the capital stocks were acquired has no effect on the current situation. The entire "mature industry" problem we've just discussed, namely the determination of output in a stationary environment, is thus side-stepped, and subsumed into the specific "profit function."

We call this "black-boxing" of the product market and all elements of the history except the levels of the capacity (or other "tangible" variable) the "state-space" assumption. The idea is that in an exceedingly complex environment, firms simplify their decision problems by only conditioning their behavior on the variables which directly influence payoffs. This "state-space" assumption greatly simplifies the analysis. It permits the use of continuous-time models, by avoiding the "curse of dimensionality": Were the strategies to depend on the entire history of play their domains would be infinite-dimensional.

As the work on competition over tangible variables is simpler than the work on mature industries and perhaps less familiar, we will examine it first and in greater detail. Section 2a reviews the continuous-time capacity-choice problem of Spence [93] and Fudenberg and Tirole [30] to introduce the idea of a state-space game and to explain the difference between precommitment ("open-loop") and perfect equilibria. Section 2 then examines two other models of the competition in tangible variables: the accumulation of "experience" and investment in advertising.

Section 3 treats three examples of competition in lumpy investments: R&D, technology adoption, and location in a growing spatial market. These examples illustrate the idea of preemption, which is an extreme form of the first-mover advantage introduced in Section 2.

Section 4 studies work by Eaton and Lipsey [24] and Maskin and Tirole [63] on entry deterrence and fixed costs in natural monopolies.

Section 5 discusses the "classic" problem of the determination of output in a mature oligopoly. We will discuss the Green and Porter paper on trigger strategies in the presence of fluctuating demand, Brock and Scheinkman on supergames with capacity constraints, and Maskin and Tirole on short-run commitments.

Section 6 discusses incomplete-information models of entry and exit. Here again we use the state-space assumption but in such models the state of the competition does not correspond to the level of a tangible variable but rather to the information each firm possesses about its rivals. In this section we discuss work on predation, limit pricing, and cutthroat competition.

2. COMPETITION IN TANGIBLE VARIABLES

2a. Introduction to state-space games

This section illustrates the use of state-space games by sketching the work of Spence [93] and Fudenberg and Tirole [30] on the use of irreversible investment as a strategic weapon. Earlier papers by Spence [92] and Dixit [20, 21] should be acknowledged, but as these assumed once-and-for-all choices of capital levels they are less suited to our expository purposes (for comprehensive treatments of barriers to entry, see also Encaoua et al. [26], Geroski and Jacquemin [37], and Von Weizsäcker [99]). Also, as we will see, the assumption that the incumbent may not invest after entry has occurred is very restrictive.

Thus, consider a duopoly, with firms indexed by $i = 1,2$. Flow profits at any time (i.e., profits gross of investment expenditures) are determined by functions $\pi^i[K_1(t), K_2(t)]$, where $K_i(t)$ is firm i's capital stock at time t. Assume that

$$\pi^i_{ii} < 0 \quad \text{and} \quad \pi^i_{ij} < 0$$

where the subscripts i, j denote partial differentiation with respect to K_i and K_j respectively.

$\Pi^i(K_i, K_j)$ is the reduced form for short-run competition, which is presumably price competition. Let us explain why the assumption $\Pi^i_{ij} < 0$, which is the basis for downward-sloping reaction curves, is fairly plausible. Capital may take two forms in our model. Either it increases capacity or it decreases costs (formally, increasing capacity is a way to decrease costs). Let us first interpret capital as capacity. Kreps and Scheinkman [53] have shown that, for a particular rationing scheme, the reduced-form profit functions did satisfy this assumption. Second, assume that capital is cost reducing, such that the unit production cost is $c^i(K_i)$. It is easy to show that for the classic model of differentiated goods on a line, the profit functions also satisfy the hypothesis. The intuition for this is that cost reductions are more advantageous the bigger the firm's market share, i.e., the higher the opponent's cost. This result seems to rely on the linearity of the demand function in prices that is peculiar to the location model. For general differentiated products, it in particular depends on the sign of second derivatives of the demand functions. By focusing on the linear case for the two interpretations of capital, we derive a presumption that the assumption $\Pi^i_{ij} < 0$ is satisfied.

It is assumed that the cost of investment (new capital) is linear, and that each firm's rate of investment, $I_i(t)$, is bounded by $\bar{I}_i$. This technology is an example of convex investment costs.

Investment must be nonnegative and there is no depreciation. Thus the capital stocks are nondecreasing. This is the key assumption—it will permit us to "work backwards" in the state space. Choose units so that $I_i(t)$ is both the rate of capital accumulation and the dollar investment in capacity. Then net profits at time t are

$$\pi^i(K_1(t), K_2(t)) - I_i(t),$$

and

$$\dot{K}_i = I_i, \; 0 \leqslant I_i \leqslant \bar{I}_i.$$

Firms maximize their time-average payoffs, so that only the eventual steady-state capital levels matter. (No firm will choose to invest forever.) Both firms enter the market at time $t = 0$ without any capital.

Let us first examine the "precommitment" or "open-loop" equilibria. In a precommitment equilibrium, firms simultaneously commit themselves to entire time-paths of investment. Thus the precommitment equilibria are really static, in that there is only one decision point for each firm. The precommitment equilibria are just like Cournot and Nash equilibria, but with a larger strategy space. In the capacity game the precommitment equilibrium is exactly the same as if both firms built their entire capital stocks at the start (because of no-discounting). In the resulting "Cournot" equilibrium each firm invests to the point at which the marginal productivity of capital equals zero, given the steady-state capital level of its opponent. There are many different paths which lead to this steady-state, all of which are precommitment equilibria. For example, each firm's strategy could be to invest as quickly as possible to its Cournot level. We can highlight the similarity of this solution to a Cournot equilibrium by defining the "steady-state reaction curves" which give each firm's desired steady-state capital level as a function of the steady-state capital level of the opposing firm. Under our assumptions, these reaction curves look the same as "nice" Cournot reactions. The reaction curves R_1 and R_2 are displayed in Figure 1. The precommitment (open-loop) equilibrium is at

$$C = (C_1, C_2),$$

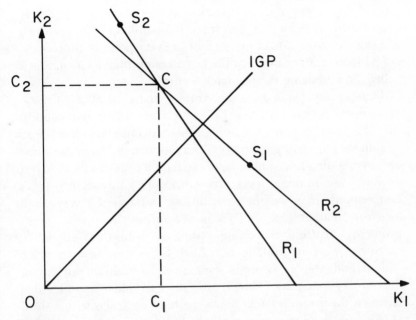

FIGURE 1   IGP = investment growth path (both firms investing as fast as possible)

the intersection of the two curves. We have seen that the use of the precommitment concept transforms an apparently dynamic game into a static one. As a modelling strategy this transformation is ill-advised. Again quoting K-S, "… one should not allow precommitment to enter by the back door … If it is possible, it should be explicitly modelled … as a formal choice in the game."

Let us next allow firm i's investment at time t to depend on the capital stocks as well as time. The capital stocks are the "state variables": the initial capital stocks and investment programs are all the information needed to compute the payoffs. A "closed-loop" equilibrium is a Nash equilibrium in state-dependent ("closed-loop") strategies. The first thing we should point out is that precommitment ("open-loop") equilibria are closed-loop equilibria. If the strategies of a firm's opponents depend only on time (and there are no random disturbances in the system), then the firm can without loss restrict itself to a strategy that depends only on time: Given the firm's optimal closed-loop strategy, the path of the system (the capital stocks at every time) is completely determined. We can then construct an open-loop strategy which calls for the same rate of investment at every point in time as the closed-loop strategy does. In the jargon of optimal control, this is called "synthesizing the feedback control."

Thus simply expanding the strategy space to allow history-dependence does not remove the "static" precommitment equilibria. Moreover, many other implausible outcomes are closed-loop equilibria. For example, firm one can threaten to "blow the game up" by building huge amounts of capacity if firm two dares invest beyond some minimal level. Given firm one's threat, firm two's best response may well be to acquiesce and accept a very small long-run market share. This is of course the "perfectness" problem—firm one is making a threat it would not choose to carry out were its bluff to be called. Of course, firms may be willing and able to commit themselves to such threats, using "doomsday machines," which are preset to inflict some terrible harm on the firm if it backs down (perhaps contracts with a third player—on this point see Schelling [82] and Gelman and Salop [36].) The point here is the same as with the open-loop strategies—to the extent that such commitments are possible they should be included in the formal model. Given such a model, we would expect that each decision that a firm makes is part of an optimal plan for the remainder of the game—bygones are bygones, except to the extent that past choices influence the current and future competitive environment. To impose this requirement we extend Selten's [87] notion of subgame perfection to state-space games in the natural way.

Definition: A set of closed-loop strategies for a state-space game is a perfect state-space equilibrium if the strategies form a closed-loop equilibrium starting from every possible initial state.

Neither of the two equilibria discussed so far is perfect. In the second equilibrium, were firm two to disregard firm one's threat and undertake nonnegligible investment, firm one would not wish to build the threatened level of capacity. In other words, the given strategies do not form an equilibrium starting from states with nonnegligible K_2. The first (precommitment) equilibrium is imperfect in a less obvious way. If both firms invest as quickly as possible, then generally one of them, say firm one, will get to its Cournot capital level before the other. The specified strategies then say that firm one should stop investing while firm two continues on to its Cournot level. But consider what would happen were firm one to deviate by investing past its Cournot level by a small amount before stopping. Firm two's strategy says that "no matter what," firm two will invest up to its Cournot level. But if firm one has already invested past C_1, then the best thing for firm two to do would be to stop on its reaction curve. The given strategies do not form a Nash equilibrium starting from states in which K_1 exceeds C_1, and so are not perfect.

The above argument suggests that the firm with the greater investment speed (or with a "headstart" in investing—the model can be extended to allow unequal entry times) can invest "strategically," that is, "overinvest" (relative to C) to reduce the investment of the other firm. Because we've assumed that such "overinvestment" is locked in (there is no depreciation or disinvestment), when presented with the fait accompli of overinvestment, the best the follower can do is take it as given when making its own decisions. With a large enough discrepancy in speeds, the "leader" can act as a Stackelberg leader, and choose its preferred point on the "follower's" reaction curve.

To see this, consider Figure 2, which depicts a perfect equilibrium. The arrows indicate the direction of motion of the state—vertical if only firm two is investing, horizontal if only firm one is investing, diagonal if each is investing as quickly as possible, and + if neither firm invests (because of the linearities, the optimal strategies are "bang-bang"). Note that we have defined choices at every state, and not just those along the equilibrium path—this is necessary in order to test for perfectness. Looking at Figure 2, we see that unless firm one has a headstart, it cannot enforce its Stackelberg outcome S_1 because it cannot accumulate enough capital before firm two reaches its reaction curve. If firm one can invest to its Stackelberg level before firm two reaches its reaction curve, it does so and then stops; firm two then continues investing up to R_2. If for some reason firm one's capital stock already exceeds its Stackelberg level, it stops immediately. The

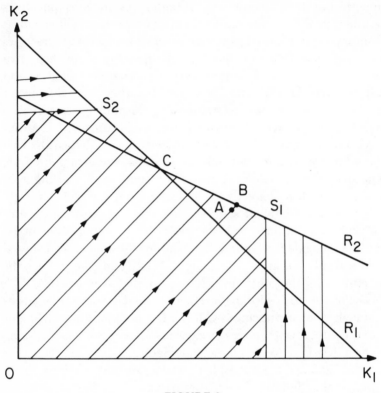

FIGURE 2

situation is symmetric on the other half of the diagram, which corresponds to states in which firm two has a headstart. Thus this equilibrium demonstrates how an advantage in investment speed or initial conditions can be exploited. The conditions of the growth phase (whose got there first, costs of adjustment, etc.) have a permanent impact on industry structure. This model also illustrates the importance of using the perfect equilibrium concept to rule out empty threats.

It turns out that the equilibrium pictured in Figure 2 is not unique. There are many others. To understand why, consider point A in Figure 2. A is close to firm two's reaction curve and past firm one's reaction curve. The strategies specify that from A on both firms invest until R_2 is reached. However, both firms would prefer the status quo at A. Firm one in particular would not

want to invest even if firm two stopped investing; it just invests in
self-defence to reduce firm two's eventual capital level. Both firms'
stopping at A is an equilibrium in the subgame starting at A,
enforced by the credible threat of going to B (or close to B) if
anyone continues investing past A. Thus the state-space restriction does not greatly restrict the set of equilibria in the investment
game.

Before going on to other models of competition over tangible
variables, we'd like to digress slightly to relate the state-space
perfectness concept to the literature on differential games and to
perfectness in games in extensive form. While perfectness is
typically explained in terms of ruling out threats, it can also
(equivalently) be motivated as the natural extension of dynamic
programming to games with more than one player. Perfectness is
just a many-player version of the principle of optimality. Thus, it
is not surprising that "perfectness" was independently formulated
by optimal-control theorists in their study of nonzerosum differential games.

Starr and Ho [95] defined a "Nash equilibrium" for a state-space
game as follows: Player i wishes to choose his control u_i to
minimize

$$\int_0^t L_i(x, u_1, \ldots u_n, t) \, \mathrm{d}t, \tag{1}$$

subject to the state evolution equation

$$\dot{x} = f(x, u_1, \ldots, u_n, t); \; x(0) = x_0 \tag{2}$$

In our capacity expansion game $x = (K_1, K_2)$, $u_i = I_i$, and $\dot{x}_i = u_i$.
For any given strategies $\tilde{u}_1(x, t)$, $\tilde{u}_2(x, t)$, the value function of the ith
player $V_i(x, t, \tilde{u})$, is just player i's payoff in the subgame starting at
(x, t) if the players play $\tilde{u}$. Using dynamic programming techniques
one can show that the value functions V_i are solutions to the partial
differential equations

$$\frac{\partial V_i}{\partial t} = \max_{u_i} H_i(x, t, u_{-i}, u_i, \partial V_i/\partial x), \tag{3}$$

where H_i, the Hamiltonian for player i, has the functional form

$$H_i(x, t, u, \lambda_i) = L_i(x, u, t) + \lambda_i f(x, u, t)$$

with
$$\lambda_i = \frac{\partial V_i}{\partial x}. \tag{4}$$

The equilibrium strategy $\tilde{u}_i$ is the control u_i which maximizes (3). To integrate (3) backwards, we must be able at each (x, t) to find the Nash equilibrium of the static game in which each player's payoff is the Hamiltonian in (4). This is not always possible. A differential game is said to be *normal* if (1), it is possible to find a *unique* instantaneous Nash equilibrium $\hat{u}$ for the payoffs H for all x, λ, and t, *and* (2), when the equations

$$\frac{\partial V_i}{\partial t} = H_i(x, t, \hat{u}, \partial V_i/\partial x) \tag{5}$$

$$\dot{x} = f(x, \hat{u}, t) \tag{6}$$

are integrated backwards from all points on the terminal surface, feasible trajectories are obtained.

Starr and Ho do prove that linear-quadratic games are "normal." Unfortunately many games of interest to economists seem not to be.

Necessary conditions for an equilibrium can also be obtained using the variational methods of optimal control theory. With the Hamiltonians defined as in (4), an equilibrium $\hat{u}$ must satisfy

$$\dot{\lambda}_i = -\frac{\partial}{\partial x} H_i(x, t, u, \lambda_i) - \sum_{j \neq i} \frac{\partial H_i}{\partial u_j} \frac{\partial \hat{u}_j}{\partial x}(x, t) \tag{7}$$

$$u_i = \hat{u}_i(x, t) \text{ maximizes } H_i(x, t, u, \lambda_i). \tag{8}$$

Notice first of all that the second term in equation (7) vanishes in a one-player game. For such a game the above conditions reduce to the familiar Hamiltonian conditions. In the n-player case, player i takes as given the strategies of his opponents. This link is captured in the second term in the co-state evolution equation, equation (7). The reason why equations (7)–(8) determine a perfect equilibrium, and not simply a closed-loop equilibrium, is that the equation is required to hold at all points in the state space, and not just those on the equilibrium path. The optimal control approach is less fruitful for n-player games than for control problems because the presence of the cross-influence term in the co-state equation transforms it from an ordinary differential equation into a system of partial differential equations, which are (much) more of a problem to solve. Throughout, Starr-Ho make one major simplifying assumption, that the value functions are smooth. While this condition can be shown to hold for control problems in "smooth" environments, it need not hold for games. This problem is a major difficulty in characterizing the set of equilibria by "integrating backwards". Again recalling the investment game, the valuation functions are discontinuous in all the "cooperative" equilibria which stop below the reaction curves— one false step by either player triggers retaliation, sending the state to the reaction curves, which is discontinuously worse than early stopping.

Perhaps as a result of the difficulties mentioned above, there have been few successful applications of differential-game techniques to economics. Reinganum's models of patent races (see, e.g. Reinganum [77]) are a conspicuous exception. However, due to the memorylessness of the games Reinganum studied, the open-loop and perfect equilibria coincide, suggesting that the games were in some sense "static." Simaan and Takayama [90] solved a differential-game model of a Cournot competition in a duopoly in which price adjusted smoothly to excess demand, i.e., instead of adjusting immediately to changes in supply, the price follows a (Walrasian) adjustment mechanism. While applications of nonzero-sum differential games are rare (see also Levine and Thépot [60] and Jørgensen [48]), we should point out that there *is* an extensive literature on zero-sum differential games, on which the control literature has concentrated—the classic example here is the game of pursuit and evasion, which has been studied with many different information structures, payoffs, and "technologies."

So far we have discussed two inclusion relationships between equilibrium concepts. We have seen that open-loop equilibria are closed-loop equilibria, and that differential games equilibria are perfect state-space equilibria. There is a third and final inclusion we should discuss in this methodological section: that between state-space perfect equilibria and the perfect equilibria of extensive-form games.

Intuitively this is clear—if the strategies of all one's opponents depend only on the payoff-relevant state, then nothing can be gained by varying one's play with other aspects of the history. Of course there may well be other perfect equilibria in which strategies do depend on the "irrelevant" history. The force of the state-space restriction is to rule out such equilibria. Clearly this restriction facilitates the analysis: indeed, it is virtually required for continuous-time games. "Extensive-form" perfectness and even Nash equilibrium are problematic in such games due to the "Aumann problem" [3] of the (uncountable) dimensionality of the domain of the strategies. But is the restriction reasonable? That depends on the context. As Kreps and Spence observe, "Implicit in (the state-space) approach is the assumption that it is the level of the tangible variables and not the way in which those levels were achieved that determines subsequent behavior and performance." Sometimes, as perhaps in the process of capital accumulation, this assumption is plausible; other times it is not. A lot depends on the complexity of the environment and the importance of the "relevant" variables. In a very complex environment the state-space restriction may be a natural heuristic for firm decisions; in a simple environment firms may be more sensitive to other aspects of the history. Similarly, if the state variables are very "important," the restriction is more plausible than if they have only a slight influence on payoffs. Taking the definition of a state-space game literally, strategies may depend on variables with arbitrarily small influence on payoffs, but not on those without any. This discontinuity can produce silly conclusions. For example, in the infinitely repeated prisoner's dilemma with complete information, the only state-space equilibrium is to always cheat. Now introduce a "state variable" which keeps track of the number of times either party has cheated. If this variable has the slightest effect on the (single-period) game, then the cooperative outcome can be supported as a state-space equilibrium. It seems unlikely that real behavior exhibits this discontinuity. The answer here is not, however, to discard the state-space formulation, but to provide a different type of reason for history to matter. State variables need not be "tangible"; intangible variables such as beliefs about the payoffs of opponents can also be payoff-relevant. Thus state-space games can be used to model history-dependence in mature industries as well as rivalry in the "immature" growth stage. In games of incomplete information the current beliefs of each firm about its opponents is the natural state variable. Here the state-space assumption requires that the history matter only to the extent that it influences those beliefs. The state-space restriction allows learning and signalling while ruling out infinite-horizon "boot-strapping," as we will see in Section 4.

2b. Oligopolies and the experience curve

Our next example of competition in tangible variables is that of oligopolies whose technologies possess an "experience curve". Our discussion is based on Fudenberg and Tirole [31]. Each firm's cost of production decreases with (individually and/or industry) cumulative output, the simplest measure of experience. Experience curves were first noticed in the manufacture of airframes in World War II and were subsequently estimated for many industries. However, many of these early studies did not use enough information to discriminate between experience effects, *static* scale economies, and exogenous technological progress. The experience curve enjoyed a brief heyday in the 1970's due to its popularisation by the Boston Consulting Group (BCG) as the key factor in strategic planning. BCG's overemphasis of the experience curve prompted a rediscovery of the shortcomings of the early empirical work, a shift to more elaborate models for strategic planning, and a general disenchantment with the experience curve itself. Nevertheless, there are some industries for which experience effects are quite important. The recent work of Lieberman [61] on the chemical processing industries found that experience effects were quite significant. Moreover, Lieberman found strong evidence for the diffusion of experience. That is, a firm's experience is not strictly proprietary, but "diffuses" to its competitors. As we will explain, the importance of this diffusion renders the "precommitment" equilibrium concept particularly inappropriate.

First, though, let us examine oligopolies whose experience curve does *not* exhibit diffusion, so that each firm's cost depends only on its own cumulative output. More precisely, let $\omega^i(t)$ denote firm i's stock of experience at time t, and let firm i's instantaneous marginal cost of production be $c[\omega^i(t)]$, so that there are constant instantaneous returns to scale. (Firm i's time-t marginal cost depends only on its experience, and not on its time-t output.) Note that the cost function $c(\cdot)$ is the same for all firms. Let $q^i(t)$ denote firm i's time-t output, $Q(t) = \sum_{i=1}^{n} q^i(t)$ and $p(q)$ is the inverse demand function. As previously, firms maximize their net present value with common discount rate r. In this game the state is simply the experience vector

$$(\omega^1(t), \ldots, \omega^n(t)).$$

So far we've been a little loose about whether the game is in discrete or continuous time. Let's specialize to continuous time for the moment to show that in a symmetric precommitment equilibrium output necessarily increases over time. Then we will show that output may decrease due to strategic considerations. So let time be continuous, with $d\omega^i/dt = q^i(t)$. For any initial experience level $\omega^i(0)$ and output path $q^i(t)$, let's define $A^i(t)$ to be the average discounted marginal cost of production from time t on:

$$A^i(t) = \int_t^\infty r \cdot \exp\left(-r(s-t)\right)c(\omega^i(s))\,ds. \qquad (9)$$

If $c(\cdot)$ were a constant from time t on, $A^i(t)$ would equal that constant. In a precommitment equilibrium, each firm chooses its output path so that $MR^i(t) = A^i(t)$ for all t, so that in some sense $A^i(t)$ is the "true" measure of firm i's marginal cost. [The effective marginal cost of production at time t is

$$c(\omega^i(t)) + \int_t^\infty \exp\left(-r(s-t)\right)c'(\omega^i(s))q^i(s)\,ds, \qquad (10)$$

where the integral term is the present value of future cost savings. Integrate this expression by parts to obtain $A^i(t)$.] Then since $A_i(t)$ is decreasing, so is marginal revenue, and in a symmetric equilibrium each firm's output is increasing. Note that this proof holds in particular for a monopolist—it illustrates a sense in which the precommitment equilibrium is like a control problem instead of a game.

In a perfect equilibrium, however, firms may wish to choose decreasing output paths. High initial output improves a firm's competitive position and may reduce the outputs of other firms.

Let us formalize perfectness in continuous time. Let $\omega(t) \equiv (\ldots, \omega^i(t), \ldots)$ denote the vector of experience levels at time t. The strategies at t depend on the current state of the game: $q^i(\omega(t))$. A differential game (Markov, state-space) equilibrium is a set of functions $\{q^i(\omega(t))\}$ such that for any time and state a firm's strategy maximizes its payoff from that time on:

$$\text{Max} \int_t^\infty \left[p\left(\sum_j q^j(\omega(s)) \right) - c(\omega^i(s)) \right] q^i(s) e^{-r(s-t)} \, ds$$

$$\text{s.t.} \quad \dot{\omega}^i(s) = q^i(s) \tag{11}$$

Writing the first order condition for this program and integrating by parts, one obtains:

$$MR(q^i(t)) = A^i(t) - \int_t^\infty p'(\textstyle\sum q^j) \left(\sum_{j \neq i} \frac{\partial q^j}{\partial \omega^i} \right) q^i(s) e^{-r(s-t)} \, ds \tag{12}$$

The interpretation is as follows: The shadow cost of output at t is equal to the open loop shadow cost (the discounted average future cost) minus the "future strategic gains from experience." A unit increase in output at time t induces a unit increase in experience at any $s > t$. This affects the rivals' outputs at time t, and therefore the market price. A perfect equilibrium is a set of functions $\{\ldots, q^i(\omega), \ldots\}$ which satisfy (11) and (12). Solving this system is a formidable task.

Since we could not solve the continuous time game, we verified the intuition that output can decrease in perfect equilibrium using a two-period model with linear demand and linear learning. That output may decrease in *asymmetric* perfect equilibrium is fairly obvious: for example, the first firm to enter a new market may produce at high volume to lower costs enough that its monopoly path from then on deters entry. It is slightly less obvious but not surprising that output may decrease even in *symmetric* perfect equilibria. We found that decreasing output is less likely if firms are impatient or there are few firms. This is intuitive: If firms are impatient the "investment incentive" of increased output is small; if firms are completely myopic the perfect and precommitment equilibria coincide. Similarly, decreasing output would not always be more likely with fewer firms, because with $n = 1$ the perfect and precommitment equilibria again coincide.

In our two-period model the "investment incentive" of increased output is simply the (discounted) change in second-period profit caused by increasing first-period output. The equations for these incentives help illustrate the difference between perfect and precommitment equilibrium. Let δ be the common discount factor, and denote the periods A and B.

In a precommitment equilibrium, the marginal investment incentive, as before, is just the marginal cost saving on future output.

$$- \delta q_B^i \frac{dc_B^i}{dq_A^i} \tag{13}$$

In a perfect equilibrium, on the other hand, each firm takes into account how its period-A output will influence the period-B outputs of its rivals. In this case the investment incentive is

$$\delta q_B^i \frac{dc_B^i}{dq_A^i} \left[-1 + p' \sum_{j \neq i} \frac{\partial q_B^j}{\partial c_B^i} \right]. \tag{14}$$

The extra term in the perfect-equilibrium investment incentive represents the indirect effect of firm i's learning on period-B price caused by the reactions of its rivals. One would expect this extra term to be positive, and in symmetric equilibria it is. This suggests that firms should produce more in the first period in perfect equilibria than in precommitment equilibria. In asymmetric cases this need not be true. Consider the example of a duopoly in which only one firm learns. This firm's first-period is greater when it takes into account the strategic effect on its rivals second-period output, so the rivals' first-period equilibrium output will be less.

Now let us examine the possibility that learning "diffuses" between firms. To model this, assume that firm i's costs depend not only on its experience but also on the total experience of its rivals. In the two-period linear case a small increase in diffusion, starting from no diffusion, decreases first-period output in perfect equilibria but increases output in precommitment equilibria. This result illustrates the importance of using the right solution concept. A firm which took the output paths of its rivals as given would be unconcerned by diffusion. As second-period costs decline with diffusion, equilibrium second-period outputs would be larger, and the incentive for cost reduction increases. Thus it is not surprising that first-period output would increase. Of course, this story assumes firms are fairly naive; they should not be eager to reduce their rivals' costs.

So far our discussion has emphasized the qualitative differences between the perfect and precommitment equilibria. Spence [94] provides numerical examples of a two-period model in which the perfect and precommitment equilibria are quantitatively similar.

Both our work and Spence's relied on quantity competition. A more promising model might be one of (pure) capacity expansion with learning. Such a model would also permit the inclusion of other types of learning effects. For example, in the petrochemical industry the capacity of a given plant often increases over time due to learning. There might also be learning effects in the *investment* technology, as in Gilbert and Harris [38].

Quantity competition must usually be seen as capacity competition, and *not* as an alternative to price competition. Instead, with the capacity interpretation, it is complementary with price competition. The exact form of this complementarity is still unknown—the papers by Fudenberg and Tirole [30], Kreps and Scheinkman [53], Maskin and Tirole [63], and Shaked and Sutton [89] envision a world in which in the medium or long run firms compete through capacities, and in which in the short run they compete through prices given these capacities. The interrelation between these variables is clearly more complex, but this is meant to formalize the idea that price changes are much more frequent (less costly) than capacity changes.

A particular drawback of the use of quantity competition to study strategic learning-by-doing (lbd) is the following: take the two-period model exposited above. In the first period firms accumulate experience to reduce their own cost in the same period, therefore reducing their opponents' second period output. A second strategic aspect is missing: the fact that firms can not only reduce their future costs by producing more, but can also increase their opponent's future costs by reducing their current market share and preventing them from learning. With quantity competition, the opponent's current output is fixed. A price competition version of the model (with differentiated products, say) would give these two effects: by reducing its price, a firm increases its market share and reduces its opponents'. The analysis would differ somewhat from that of Fudenberg and Tirole. The reason for overinvesting in lbd would not be to reduce one's own costs (high costs are not a disadvantage in price competition because reaction curves are upward sloping), but to increase one's opponents' costs. The choice of formalizing capacity on price competition eventually boils down to the kind of learning one would expect (through investment or through production). This point has important consequences for competitive strategy: If one believes in capacity competition, reducing one's own cost is the crucial element; if one believes that price competition is more relevant, increasing the opponent' cost matters. The two are not equivalent since they depend on the relative technologies of the firms.   Let us examine the consequences of price competition in our two-period model of lbd. The period B effect of a unit change in firm i's period A price p_A^i is

$$\delta\left[\frac{\mathrm{d}\Pi_B^i}{\mathrm{d}c_B^i}\frac{\mathrm{d}c_B^i}{\mathrm{d}D_A^i}\frac{\partial D_A^i}{\partial p_A^i} + \frac{\mathrm{d}\Pi_B^i}{\mathrm{d}c_B^j}\frac{\mathrm{d}c_B^j}{\mathrm{d}D_A^j}\frac{\partial D_A^j}{\partial p_A^i}\right] \tag{15}$$

where $D_A^i(p_A^i, p_A^j)$ is the first period demand for firm i's product and $\Pi_B^i(c_B^i, c_B^j)$ is the reduced form for profits after solving for period B price competition. This expression says that i's period A price influences i's and j's period A outputs, and thus period B unit costs, and hence affects firm i's period B profit.

We know that $\mathrm{d}c_B^i/\mathrm{d}D_A^i < 0$, $\mathrm{d}c_B^j/\mathrm{d}D_A^j < 0$ (lbd), $\partial D_A^i/\partial p_A^i < 0$, $\partial D_A^j/\partial p_A^i > 0$ and $\mathrm{d}\Pi_B^i/\mathrm{d}c_B^j > 0$. The last term to sign is $\mathrm{d}\Pi_B^i/\mathrm{d}c_B^i$. A unit change in c_B^i has two effects. It increases costs by D_B^i, and it increases firm j's price (since the reaction curves in general are upward sloping). These effects go in opposite directions, but it seems plausible that overall firm i's profit decreases with its costs:

$d\Pi_B^i/dc_B^i < 0$. This is indeed the case, for example, in the classic location problem on a circle or a line. Thus we conclude that the expression given by (14) is negative, so firms have a dynamic incentive to produce more. As with investing in capital accumulation (described in the previous model), a firm may have less incentive to learn in perfect equilibrium than in open-loop equilibrium: imagine that firm j does not learn so that the second term in (14) is zero. Then the difference between the open-loop and perfect incentives is the effect that c_B^i has on p_B^j in perfect equilibrium. But we know that a low c_B^i induces firm j to choose a low p_B^j and hence indirectly hurts firm i.

2c. The fat-cat effect and the lean and hungry look

In the previous models of strategic investment (capital accumulation and learning-by-doing), firms "overaccumulated" capital to induce "timider" behavior by their rivals—i.e., less investment or output. This section points out that in some cases being big may be a handicap, because it may reduce the incentive to respond aggressively to competitors. In such circumstances firms may choose to maintain a "lean and hungry look" by under-accumulating capital, thus avoiding the "fat-cat effects." We also provide a taxonomy of the incentives for strategic investment by an incumbent.

Our examples show that the key factors are whether investment makes the incumbent more or less "tough" in the post-entry game, and how the entrant reacts to tougher play by the incumbent. These two factors are the basis of our taxonomy. Bulow, Geanakoplos, and Klemperer [13] have independently noted the importance of the entrant's reaction.

In our advertising model, a customer can buy from a firm only if he is aware of its existence. To inform consumers, firms place ads in newspapers. An ad that is read informs the customer of the existence of the firm and also gives the firm's price. In the first period only the incumbent is in the market; in the second period the entrant may enter. The crucial assumption is that some of the customers who received an ad in the first period do not bother to read the ads in the second period, and therefore buy only from the incumbent. This captive market for the incumbent represents the incumbent's accumulation of goodwill. One could derive such captivity from a model in which rational consumers possess imperfect information about product quality, as in Schmalensee [85], or from a model in which customers must sink firm-specific costs in learning how to consume the product.

As we shall see, the incumbent will underinvest in advertising if it chooses to deter entry, because by lowering its stock of "goodwill" it establishes a credible threat to cut prices in the event of entry. Conversely, if the established firm chooses to allow entry, it will advertise heavily and become a fat cat in order to soften the entrant's pricing behavior. Thus the strategic inventives for investment depend on whether or not the incumbent chooses to deter entry. This contrasts with previous work on strategic investment in which the strategic incentives always encourage the incumbent to overaccumulate capital.

There are two firms, an incumbent (1) and an entrant (2), and a unit population of ex-ante identical consumers. If a consumer is aware of both firms, and the incumbent charges x_1, and the entrant charges x_2, the consumer's demands for the two goods are $D^1(x_1, x_2)$ and $D^2(x_1, x_2)$ respectively. If a consumer is only aware of the incumbent (entrant), his demand is $D^1(x_1, \infty)$ $(D^2(\infty, x_2))$. The (net of variable costs) revenue an informed consumer brings the incumbent is $R^1(x_1, x_2)$ or $R^1(x_1, \infty)$ depending on whether the consumer also knows about the entrant or not, and similarly for the entrant. We'll assume that the revenues are differentiable, quasi-concave in own prices, and they, as well as the marginal revenue, increase with the competitor's price (these are standard assumptions for price competition with differentiated goods).

To inform consumers, the firms put ads in the newspapers. An ad that is read makes the customer aware of the product and gives the price. The cost of reaching a fraction K of the population in the first period is $A(K)$, where $A(K)$ is convex for strictly positive levels of advertising, and $A(1) = \infty^2$. There are two periods,

---

2. See Butters [14] and Grossman and Shapiro [42] for examples of advertising technologies. Note that we do not rule out the possibility of a fixed cost of advertising.

$t = 1, 2$. In the first period only the incumbent is in the market. It advertises K_1, charges the monopoly price and makes profits $K_1 \cdot R^m$ where R^m is the monopoloy profit. In the second period the entrant may enter.

To further simplify, we assume that all active firms will choose to cover the remaining market in the second period at cost A_2. Then assuming entry, the profits of the two firms, Π^1 and Π^2 can be written:

$$\Pi^1 = [-A(K_1) + K_1 R^m] + \delta[K_1 R^1(x_1, \infty)$$
$$+ (1 - K_1)R^1(x_1, x_2) - A_2]$$
$$\Pi^2 = \delta[(1 - K_1)R^2(x_1, x_2) - A_2], \qquad (16)$$

where δ is the common discount factor.

In the second period, the firms simultaneously choose prices. Assuming that Nash equilibrium for this second-stage game exists and is characterized by the first-order conditions, we have

$$K_1 R^1_1(x^*_1, \infty) + (1 - K_1)R^1_1(x^*_1, x^*_2) = 0; \qquad (17)$$

$$R^2_2(x^*_1, x^*_2) = 0, \qquad (18)$$

where $R^i_j = \partial R^i(x_1, x_2)/\partial x_j$, and x^*_i is the equilibrium value of x_i as a function of K_1.

From equation (17), and the assumption that $R^i_{ij} > 0$, we see that

$$R^1_1(x^*_1, \infty) > 0 > R^1_1(x^*_1, x^*_2).$$

The incumbent would like to increase its price for its captive customers, and reduce it where there is competition; but price discrimination has been assumed impossible.

Differentiating the first-order conditions, and using $R^i_{ij} > 0$, we have

$$\partial x^*_1/\partial K_1 > 0, \ \partial x^*_1/\partial x^*_2 > 0, \ \partial x^*_2/\partial K_1 = 0, \ \partial x^*_2/\partial x^*_1 > 0. \quad (19)$$

The heart of the fat-cat effect is that $\partial x^*_1/\partial K_1 > 0$. As the incumbent's goodwill increases it becomes more reluctant to match the entrant's price. The large captive market makes the incumbent a pacifistic "fat cat." This suggests that if entry is going to occur, the incumbent has an incentive to increase K_1 to "soften" the second-period equilibrium.

To formalize this intuition we first must sign the *total* derivative dx_1^*/dK_1. While one would expect increasing K_1 to increase the incumbent's equilibrium price, this is only true if firm one's second-period reaction curve is steeper than firm two's. This will be true if $R_{11}^1 \cdot R_{22}^2 > R_{12}^1 \cdot R_{21}^2$. If dx_1^*/dK_1 were negative the model would not exhibit the fat-cat effect.

Now we compare the first-order conditions for the incumbent's choice of K_1 in the open-loop and perfect equilibria. In the open-loop equilibrium, the incumbent takes x_2^* as given in choosing K_1, and thus ignores the possibility of strategic investment. Setting $\partial \Pi^1/\partial K_1 = 0$ in (16) yields

$$R^m + \delta(R^1(x_1^*, \infty) - R^1(x_1^*, x_2^*)) = A'(K_1). \qquad (20)$$

In perfect equilibrium, the incumbent realizes that x_2^* depends on K_1, giving first-order conditions $d\Pi^1/dK_1 = 0$,

$$R^m + \delta \left(R^1(x_1^*, \infty) - R^1(x_1^*, x_2^*) + (1 - K_1)R_2^1 \frac{dx_2^*}{dK_1} \right) = A'(K_1). \qquad (21)$$

As R_2^1 and dx_2^*/dK_1 are positive, for a fixed K_1 the left-hand side of (21) exceeds that of (20), so if the second-order condition corresponding to (21) is satisfied, its solution exceeds that of (20).

The fat-cat effect suggests a corollary, that the incumbent should underinvest and maintain a "lean and hungry look" to deter entry. However, while the "price effect" of increasing K_1 encourages entry, the "direct effect" of reducing the entrant's market goes the other way. To see this, note that

$$\Pi_{K_1}^2 = \delta \left[(1 - K_1)R_1^2 \frac{dx_1^*}{dK_1} - R^2 \right]. \qquad (22)$$

The first term in the right-hand side of (21) is the strategic effect of K_1 on the second-period price, the second is the direct effect. One can find plausible examples of demand and advertising functions such that the indirect effect dominates. This is the case for example for goods which are differentiated by their location on the unit interval, with linear "transportation" costs, if first-period advertising is sufficiently expensive that the incumbent's equilibrium share of the informed consumers is positive. In this case entry deterrence requires underinvestment.

We now develop a simple model of investment in R&D to illustrate the lean and hungry look, building on the work of Arrow [2] and Reinganum [78]. In the first period, the incumbent, firm one, spends K_1 on "capital," and then has constant average cost $\bar{c}(K_1)$. The incumbent receives the monopoly profit $V^m(\bar{c}(K_1))$ in period 1. In the second period, both the incumbent and firm two may do R&D on a new technology which allows constant average cost c. If only one firm succeeds in developing the new technology, its profit is $V^m(c)$. Thus the innovation is "large" or "drastic" in Arrow's sense. If both firms develop the innovation, their profit is zero, because the technology is to be sold to a user who can bid the price down to the competitive level if both discover. If neither firm succeeds, then the incumbent again receives $V^m(\bar{c})$. The second-period R&D technology is stochastic. If firm i spends x_i on R&D, it obtains the new technology with probability $\mu_i(x_i)$. We assume $\mu_i'(0) = \infty$, $\mu_i' > 0$, $\mu_i'' < 0$. The total payoffs from period 2 on are:

$$\Pi^1 = \mu_1(1 - \mu_2)V^m(c) + (1 - \mu_1)(1 - \mu_2)V^m(\bar{c}) - x_1$$
$$\Pi^2 = \mu_2(1 - \mu_1)V^m(c) - x_2. \tag{23}$$

The first-order conditions for a Nash equilibrium are:

$$\mu_1'[V^m(c) - V^m(\bar{c})][1 - \mu_2] = 1$$
$$\mu_2'V^m(c)(1 - \mu_1) = 1. \tag{24}$$

We see that since the incumbent's gain is only the difference in the monopoly profits, it has less incentive to innovate than the entrant. This is the "Arrow effect." We have derived it here in a model with each firm's chance of succeeding independent of the other's, so that we have had to allow a nonzero probability of a tie. Reinganum's model, discussed in Section 3, avoids ties because of its continuous-time nature.

Because $\mu_i' > 0$ and $\mu_i'' < 0$, the reaction curves in (24) slope downward—the more one firm spends, the less the other wishes to. Since increasing K_1 decreases the incumbent's gain from the innovator's, we expect that the strategic incentive is to reduce K_1

to play more aggressively in period 2. As in our last example, this is only true if the reaction curves are "stable," which in this case requires $\mu_1''\mu_2''(1 - \mu_1)(1 - \mu_2) > (\mu_1'\mu_2')^2$, which is true for example for $\mu_i(x) = \max(1, b\sqrt{x})$, with b small. We conclude that to accommodate entry the incumbent has a strategic incentive to underinvest. Because K_1 has no direct effect on Π^2, we can also say that to deter entry the incumbent has an incentive to underinvest.[3]

In the goodwill model the incumbent could underinvest to deter entry, while in the R&D model the strategic incentives always favor underinvestment. To relate these results to previous work, we next present an informal taxonomy of pre-entry strategic investment by an incumbent. In many cases, one might expect both "investment" and "production" decisions to be made post-entry. We have restricted attention to a single post-entry variable for simplicity. We should point out that this involves some loss of generality. Strategic underinvestment requires that the incumbent not be able to invest after entry, or more generally that pre-entry and post-entry investments are imperfectly substitutable. This was the case in both of our examples. However, if investment is in productive machinery and capital costs are linear and constant over time, then underinvestment would be ineffective, as the incumbent's postentry investment would make up any previous restraint.

Before presenting the taxonomy, which is original, we should acknowledge that since Schmalensee's [86] article several authors have independently noticed the possibility of underinvestment. Baldani [5] studies that conditions leading to underinvestment in advertising. Bulow, Geanakoplos, and Klemperer [13] present a careful treatment of two-stage games in which either production or investment takes place in the first period, with production in the second, and costs need not be separable across periods. They focus on cost minimization as the benchmark for over- and under-investment. The starting point for the Bulow, Geanakoplos and Klemperer paper was the observation that a firm might choose not to enter an apparently profitable

---

3. For small innovations the direct effect goes the other way.

market due to strategic spillovers on other product lines. This point is developed in more detail in Judd [49].

Our taxonomy classifies market according to the signs of the incentives for strategic investments. Because only the incumbent has a strategic incentive, given concavity in the case of entry accommodation we can unambiguously say whether the incumbent will over- or underinvest (compared to the open-loop equilibrium).[4] We continue to denote the incumbent's first-period choice K_1, the post-entry decisions x_1 and x_2, and the payoffs Π^1 and Π^2. For entry deterrence there are two effects, as we noted before: the "direct effect" $\partial \Pi^2 / \partial K_1$, and the "strategic effect" $\partial \Pi^2 / \partial x_1^* \cdot \partial x_1^* / \partial K_1$. We saw in the goodwill case that these two effects had opposite signs, and so the overall incentives were ambiguous. In all the rest of our examples, these two effects have the same sign.

In each component of the grid we give first the entry-accommodating strategy and then the entry-deterring one. The "fat-cat" strategy is overinvestment that accommodates entry by committing the incumbent to play less aggressively post-entry. The "lean and hungry" strategy is underinvestment to be tougher. The "top dog" strategy is overinvestment to be tough; this is the familiar result of Spence and Dixit.

Last, the "puppy-dog" strategy is *underinvestment* that accommodates entry by turning the incumbent into a small, friendly, nonaggressive puppy dog. This strategy is desirable if investment makes the incumbent tougher, and the second-period reaction curves slope up.

One final caveat: the classification in Table 1 depends as previously on the second-period Nash equilibria being "stable," so that changing K_1 has the intuitive effect on x_2^*.

Our goodwill model is an example of Case I: goodwill makes

---

4. This does not generalize to the case in which both firms make strategic decisions. In our paper on learning-by-doing (Fudenberg and Tirole [32]) we give an example in which one firm's first-period output declined in moving from the precommitment to the perfect equilibrium. The problem is that if, as expected, firm one's output increases when it plays strategically, firm two's strategic incentive to increase output can be outweighed by its response to firm one's change.

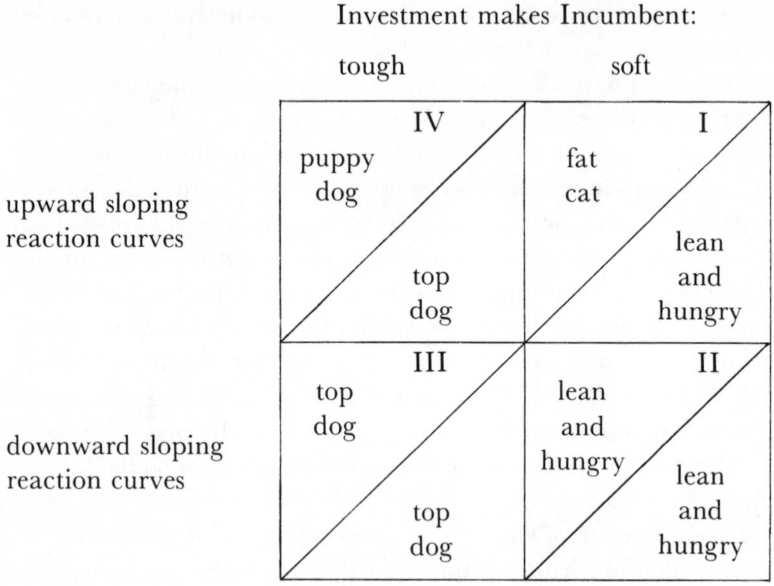

Investment makes Incumbent:

tough   soft

upward sloping reaction curves	IV puppy dog ╱ top dog	I fat cat ╱ lean and hungry
downward sloping reaction curves	III top dog ╱ top dog	II lean and hungry ╱ lean and hungry

FIGURE 3

the incumbent soft, and the second-period reaction curves slope up. The R&D model illustrates Case II. Case III is the "classic" case for investing in productive machinery and "learning by doing" with quantity competition. Case IV results from either of these models with price competition. A more novel example of the puppy-dog ploy arises in the Milgrom and Roberts [67] model of limit pricing under incomplete information, if we remove their assumption that the established firm's cost is revealed once the entrant decides to enter, and replace quantity with price as the strategic variable. To accommodate entry, the incumbent then prefers the entrant to believe that the incumbent's costs are relatively high.

We conclude this section with the warning that the two-period models we have just examined rule out the strategic interactions we discussed in Section 2a. As we saw there, these interactions may reverse to over- or under-investment results: investment in productive machinery is a "top-dog" game in our taxonomy, but in a multistage game the steady-state capital levels can be below those of open-loop equilibria.

3. PREEMPTION

Section 2 examined competition in continuous (divisible) investments such as learning and goodwill. Many investments, however, are discrete (lumpy) and the first mover advantage described in section 2 takes an extreme form, that of preemption.
This section treats three examples of competition in lumpy
investments. Two of them, the adoption of a new technology and
location in a growing spatial market, are classic instances of such
investments. In the third example, R&D, the firm's investment
(research expenditures) and its outcome (the discovery of a new
technology) differ in that, to some extent, the investment is
continuous while its outcome is lumpy. Because the effects of the
R&D outcome on market structure and payoffs closely resembles
those of lumpy investments, we study R&D, adoption, and
location models in the same section. As in section 2c, we formulate
the models in terms of an incumbent (firm one) and an entrant
(firm two).

(a) *R&D*

The persistence of monopoly debate   We begin our discussion of
R&D by summarizing the *American Economic Review* exchange
between Gilbert and Newberry [39] and Reinganum [78] on the
persistence of monopoly. Consider a continuous time race for a
patent between an entrant and an incumbent. The existing
technology, patented by the incumbent, allows production at unit
cost $\bar{c}$, with corresponding monopoly profit per unit of time of
$\Pi_0^m (> 0)$. The (fixed and known) new technology, to be patented
by either the incumbent or the entrant, will allow production at
unit cost $c < \bar{c}$. If the incumbent innovates first, it makes profit
$\Pi_1^m (> \Pi_0^m)$ per unit of time. If the entrant innovates first, it makes
$\Pi_2^d (> 0)$ and the incumbent $\Pi_1^d (\geqslant 0)$. We assume that
$\Pi_1^m \geqslant \Pi_1^d + \Pi_2^d$, that is a monopoly can always do as well as two
uncoordinated firms.

Following Loury [62], Dasgupta and Stiglitz [18], Lee and
Wilde [57], and Reinganum [77, 78], let us assume that the time
to discovery is a Poisson process. If a firm spends $x\,dt$ between t and

$(t + dt)$, its probability of discovery in that period of time is $h(x)dt$, where h is an increasing function which is the same for both firms. Notice that the probability of discovery at any time depends only on current expenditures, and not on past ones. Thus in the terminology of section 2 there is no "capital" or state variable. This memorylessness, coupled with stationarity, implies that we can restrict attention to "static" strategies in which the expenditures (x_1, x_2) are constant over time (until someone gets the patent). The expected payoffs to (x_1, x_2) are

$$V_1 = \frac{h(x_1)\Pi_1^m/r + h(x_2)\Pi_1^d/r + \Pi_0^m - x_1}{r + h(x_1) + h(x_2)}$$

and

$$V_2 = \frac{h(x_2)\Pi_2^d/r - x_2}{r + h(x_1) + h(x_2)},$$

where r is the common rate of interest.

These payoff functions illustrate two differences between the incumbent's and the entrant's incentives to do R&D. First, notice that $\frac{\partial}{\partial \Pi_0^m}\left(\frac{\partial V_1}{\partial x_1}\right) < 0$, so increasing the incumbent's pre-innovation profit reduces its incentive to do R&D. This is the familiar Arrow (1962) "replacement effect". It tends to lower the incumbent's R & D expenditures compared to the entrant's, who has no pre-innovation profits. Second, the "preemptive" payoff to innovation, that is the difference in payoff between winning the patent and letting the rival win it, is bigger for the incumbent than for the entrant. The latter's preemptive payoff is Π_2^d, while the incumbent's is $(\Pi_1^m - \Pi_1^d) \geqslant \Pi_2^d$. This effect is emphasized by Gilbert and Newberry [39] and will be called the "efficiency effect". The incumbent has more incentive to innovate because a monopoly is more efficient (in making profits).

Either of these effects can dominate. For example if the innovation is "drastic" in Arrow's sense, $(c \ll \bar{c})$ so that if the entrant innovates first it becomes a *de facto* monopoly, then $\Pi_2^d = \Pi_1^m$ and there is no "efficiency effect". In this case the entrant will spend more, as confirmed by Reinganum's analysis.

On the other hand, under Bertrand competition, if c is close to $\bar{c}$, then we can show that either the entrant or the incumbent can spend more on R&D, depending on the technology. In particular, assume that $h(x) = x^\alpha$, $0 < \alpha < 1$, so that $xh(x)$ goes to zero as x does. For a small innovation, $h(x_1)$ and $h(x_2)$ will be small compared to the interest rate r, and the entrant's first-order condition is approximately $\alpha x_2^{\alpha-1} \Pi_2^d \sim r$, or $x_2 \sim \left(\dfrac{\alpha \Pi_2^d}{r} \right)^{1/(1-\alpha)}$.

Thus since Π_2^d is of order $\Delta c = \bar{c} - c$, x_2 is of order $(\Delta c)^{1/(1-\alpha)}$. The incumbent's first-order condition is approximately

$$\alpha x_1^{\alpha-1} \left[(\Pi_1^m - \Pi_0^m) + (\alpha \Pi_2^d/r)^{\alpha/(1-\alpha)} \frac{\Pi_1^m}{r} \right] \sim r,$$

where we have substituted for $h(x_2)$. The first term inside the square brackets is the incumbent's incentive to replace itself; the second is its incentive to avoid preemption. We expect that if the replacement term dominates, the incumbent spends less on R&D than the entrant does, while if the preemption term dominates, the incumbent spends more. It turns out that this intuition is correct. The first case corresponds to $\alpha > \frac{1}{2}$, and the second to $\alpha < \frac{1}{2}$. To see this, first note that $(\Pi_1^m - \Pi_0^m)$ and Π_2^d are of the same order in Δc. Indeed, $(\Pi_1^m - \Pi_0^m) \sim D(p^m(\bar{c}))\Delta c$, where $D(\cdot)$ denotes the demand function and $p^m(\cdot)$ the monopoly price; and, under Bertrand competition, $\Pi_2^d = D(\bar{c})\Delta c$. If $\alpha < \frac{1}{2}$, the preemption term dominates the replacement term in the square brackets. So x_1 is of order $(\Delta c)^{\alpha/(1-\alpha)^2}$, while x_2 is of order $(\Delta c)^{1/(1-\alpha)}$. Hence x_1/x_2 goes to infinity when Δc goes to zero. If $\alpha > \frac{1}{2}$, the replacement term dominates, and $x_1 \sim (\alpha(\Pi_1^m - \Pi_0^m)/r)^{1/(1-\alpha)}$. Since $\Pi_1^m - \Pi_0^m < \Pi_2^d$, $x_1 < x_2$. Thus we see that what matters is the behavior of the entrant's equilibrium hazard rate, $h(x_2)$, as Δc goes to zero. If $h(x_2)$ goes to zero sufficiently quickly, the incumbent is unconcerned by preemption, and expenditures are the same as if each firm ignored the presence of its rival. If $h(x_2)$ shrinks more slowly, then the incumbent is concerned by preemption even for very small innovations.

We can also examine what happens when there is "little uncertainty" in the R&D technology. There are several ways to formalize this notion. Let us give two:

First one can assume that to discover at some time T (with probability one) each firm must spend some fixed amount of money that decreases with T. This is the approach taken by Gilbert and Newberry. It has the disadvantage of not formalizing the R&D process explicity. It is very akin to the models of adoption and location with Bertrand competition described below. This type of model easily generates persistence of monopoly, a result radically opposed to Reinganum's (see 3d though).

Second one can study the limit equilibrium for a family of stochastic R&D technologies such that the date of discovery becomes deterministic. A slight problem with memoryless technologies is that the limit date of deterministic discovery must be 0. It is nevertheless instructive to note that even with these technologies the replacement effect disappears as the uncertainty shrinks, so that the efficiency effect dominates. To show this, consider an initial memoryless technology $h(x)$, where h is increasing and concave, and define the family of memoryless technologies $\lambda h\left(\dfrac{x}{\lambda}\right)$ for $\lambda > 1$. These functions are concave transforms of h. When λ increases, the technology becomes more and more "linear", so that the date of discovery will converge to 0. Straightforward computations show that, as λ goes to infinity, $\tilde{x}_1 \equiv \dfrac{x_1}{\lambda}$ and $\tilde{x}_2 \equiv \dfrac{x_2}{\lambda}$ are given (approximately) by the two equations:

$$h'(\tilde{x}_1)\left(h(\tilde{x}_2)\left(\frac{\Pi_1^m - \Pi_1^d}{r}\right) + \tilde{x}_1\right) \simeq h'(\tilde{x}_2)\left(h(\tilde{x}_1)\frac{\Pi_2^d}{r} + \tilde{x}_2\right)$$

$$\simeq h(\tilde{x}_1) + h(\tilde{x}_2). \qquad (25)$$

(25) implies that $\tilde{x}_1 > \tilde{x}_2$, so that the incumbent invests more when there is little uncertainty.[5]

---

5. (25) and the convexity of h imply that $h'(\tilde{x}_1)\left(\dfrac{\Pi_1^m - \Pi_1^d}{r}\right) > 1$. Then fix $\tilde{x}_1$ and consider $F(\tilde{x}_2) \equiv$ LHS of (25)—RHS of (25). In a Nash equilibrium one must have $F(\tilde{x}_2) = 0$. Note that $F(\tilde{x}_2) \geqslant 0$ as $(\Pi_1^m - \Pi_1^d) \geqslant \Pi_2^d$. If $F'(\tilde{x}_2) > 0$ whenever $F(\tilde{x}_2) = 0$, then we are done. But

$$F'(\tilde{x}_2) = h'(\tilde{x}_1)h'(\tilde{x}_2)\frac{\Pi_1^m - \Pi_1^d}{r} - h''(\tilde{x}_2)\left(h(\tilde{x}_1)\frac{\Pi_2^d}{r} + \tilde{x}_2\right) - h'(\tilde{x}_2)$$

$$> h'(\tilde{x}_2)\left(h'(\tilde{x}_1)\frac{\Pi_1^m - \Pi_1^d}{r} - 1\right) > 0.$$

The R&D models provide another illustration of a fat-cat effect: Imagine that the incumbent has a (pre-entry) choice of the initial cost $\bar{c}$. Reducing $\bar{c}$ by spending more before entry increases Π_0^m and reduces the incumbent's willingness to do R&D. Furthermore, in the post-entry game the reaction curves are upward sloping: An increase in x_1 hastens the expected date of discovery by firm one, and therefore induces firm two to invest more to be first. So in its pre-entry behavior (choice of initial technology), the incumbent overinvests and voluntarily becomes a fat cat[6].

Experience and preemption in patent races   In the memoryless models described above, patent competition is unending (indeed, constant) until the time of discovery. If instead the R&D process does have a memory, so that the probability of discovery at a given date depends on *past* expenditures, then entry deterrence through capital accumulation (the "top-dog" strategy) becomes feasible. As in section 2, whether an incumbent chooses to deter entry depends on the cost structure of investments. (For examples of R&D technologies that generate entry barriers, see Dasgupta and Stiglitz [18], Fudenberg, Gilbert, Stiglitz and Tirole [28, model 1], and Harris and Vickers [44].

The stochastic nature of R&D allows patent competition to exhibit other intermediate types of dynamic market configuration. In some cases firms may compete for a while and then give up before discovery. Obvious examples are if the probability of discovery falls over time (no news is bad news) or if the value of the patent decreases over time (perhaps due to the existence of a future backstop technology). The examples above are based on "declining" markets, and would yield "intermediate" competition even if the R&D technology were memoryless. More generally, intermediate competition can occur in stationary or improving markets if past R&D expenditures matter. In that case, patent competition takes on the characteristics of a race, and

---

6. This last conclusion differs from the one in our R&D model of Section 2c. There R&D did not involve preemption, because firms did not learn if the other had succeeded before the end of their own R&D program.

we can speak of firms being "ahead" or "behind" in terms of their expected probability of winning if all firms incur the same costs. Then, as shown in Fudenberg, Gilbert, Stiglitz and Tirole, the key to "intermediate" outcomes to the patent race is whether a firm that is behind can "leapfrog" discontinuously into the lead. First, the link between expenditure and the "experience" or capital variable that determines each firm's position in the race may be stochastic, as in a multistage patent race in which a number of intermediate discoveries must be made in sequence before work can begin on a patentable technology. In this case the current leader in the race may become discouraged and drop out if an opponent makes an intermediate discovery. Second, information about the firm's R&D expenditures need not be perfect. This allows a firm to leapfrog into the lead before the leader can react, because the leader cannot ensure that it is matching its rivals' expenditures. Fudenberg, Gilbert, Stiglitz and Tirole formalized this intuition in a discrete-time model. Such models are a very rough way to study imperfect information. Continuous-time models with information lags would be more satisfactory but have not been developed. So far, only the two extreme cases of continuous-time models of imperfect information have been studied: open loop strategies, which correspond to infinite lags in information, and the strategies in Fudenberg and Tirole [31] which correspond to negligible information lags. A final possible reason for firms to compete for a while and then leave is that firms have private information about their own R&D technology. This idea is a special case of the model of exit sketched in section 6.

(b) Preemption and the adoption of a new technology

We next look at preemption in the adoption of new technologies, as opposed to their creation. Here a deterministic link between expenditures and outcomes seems more reasonable.

Imagine now that the incumbent starts with technology $\bar{c}$; that an innovation, which lowers the production cost down to c, becomes available at date 0; and that each firm's only decision is the choice of its date of adoption. The innovation is publicly available, and adopting it costs a fixed amount $f(t)$ where $f(t)$ is decreasing and convex. f is "high" at date 0 (no one wants to adopt initially) and eventually becomes "low" (both firms will end up adopting). The incumbent starts with profit $\Pi_0^m (> 0)$ per unit of time (and the entrant 0). If only the incumbent has adopted it makes profit $\Pi_1^m (> \Pi_0^m)$ per unit of time (and the entrant 0). If only the entrant has adopted, the firms make profit Π_1^d and Π_2^d per unit of time respectively, with $\Pi_1^d + \Pi_2^d \leqslant \Pi_1^m$. And if both firms have adopted they make identical profits Π^d per unit of time, with $\Pi_1^d < \Pi^d < \Pi_2^d$.

If the incumbent adopts first at t_1 and the entrant follows at $t_2 \geqslant t_1$, the incumbent's net present value is:

$$V_1 = \int_0^{t_1} \Pi_0^m e^{-rt} \mathrm{d}t + \int_{t_1}^{t_2} \Pi_1^m e^{-rt} \mathrm{d}t + \int_{t_2}^{\infty} \Pi^d e^{-rt} \mathrm{d}t - f(t_1) e^{-rt_1}$$

and the entrant's:

$$V_2 = \int_{t_2}^{\infty} \Pi^d e^{-rt} \mathrm{d}t - f(t_2) e^{-rt_2}$$

where r is the common rate of interest.

If the entrant adopts first at t_1 and the incumbent follows at t_2, the two payoffs become:

$$V_1 = \int_0^{t_1} \Pi_0^m e^{-rt} \mathrm{d}t + \int_{t_1}^{t_2} \Pi_1^d e^{-rt} \mathrm{d}t + \int_{t_2}^{\infty} \Pi^d e^{-rt} \mathrm{d}t - f(t_2) e^{-rt_2}$$

and:

$$V_2 = \int_{t_1}^{t_2} \Pi_2^d e^{-rt} \mathrm{d}t + \int_{t_2}^{\infty} \Pi^d e^{-rt} \mathrm{d}t - f(t_1) e^{-rt_1}.$$

Note that if the incumbent has already adopted at t_1, the optimal date of adoption for the entrant is:

$$t_2 = \max \, (t_1, \, T_2^F) \text{ where } - \Pi^d e^{-rT_2^F} - (f(T_2^F) e^{-rT_2^F})' \equiv 0. \quad (26)$$

Similarly if the entrant preempts at t_1, the optimal date of adoption for the incumbent is

$$t_2 = \max \, (t_1, \, T_1^F) \text{ where } - (\Pi^d - \Pi_1^d) e^{-rT_1^F} - (f(T_1^F) e^{-rT_1^F})' \equiv 0.$$
$$(27)$$

Clearly $T_1^F > T_2^F$, so the entrant is a "faster second". This is due to the fact that it does not make a duopoly profit before adoption.

If any firm adopts first, it can anticipate the other firm's reaction. Taking this into account allows us to define payoffs to the incumbent and the entrant of adopting first at t_1, $L_1(t_1)$ and $L_2(t_1)$, or to be preempted at t_1, $F_1(t_1)$ and $F_2(t_1)$.

To derive these "leader/follower curves" L_i and F_i, we must pin down the relationships between the various flow profits by specifying the nature of the competition in the product market. We here give two such specifications to highlight the main issues.

Let us first assume that firms are *Bertrand competitors* in the product market, and that their products are perfect substitutes. Let $\pi^m(c) = \max_p \{(p - c)D(p)\}$. Before adoption, the incumbent earns $\pi_0^m = \pi^m(\bar{c})$ per unit of time. Let us now consider what happens once one of the firms has adopted the new technology. An important feature of Bertrand competition is that the follower never adopts, i.e., $T_1^F = T_2^F = +\infty$, as variable profits are driven down to zero by price competition and cannot amortize the adoption cost. Note also that $\pi_1^d = \pi^d = 0$.

Figure 4 then completely summarizes the adoption game.

Let T_1 and T_2 denote the (first) times such that the incumbent and the entrant are indifferent between being the leader and being the follower:

$$L_1(T_1) \equiv F_1(T_1); \quad L_2(T_2) = F_2(T_2).$$

T_1 and T_2 are given by:

$$\frac{\pi^m(c)}{r} = f(T_1)$$

and

$$\frac{\pi_2^d}{r} = f(T_2).$$

A drastic innovation is such that $\pi_2^d = \pi^m(c)$. For a non-drastic innovation, $\pi_2^d = (\bar{c} - c)D(\bar{c}) < < \pi^m(c)$. We thus see that $T_1 \leq T_2$, with equality only if the innovation is drastic. Figure 4 is drawn for the non-drastic case.

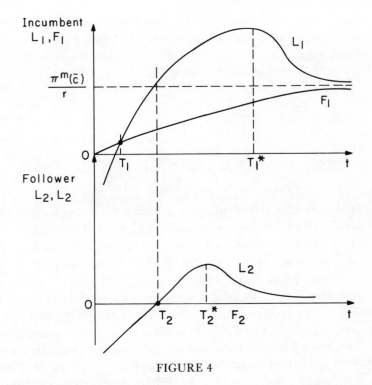

FIGURE 4

Let us consider the non-drastic case. Let T_i^* denote the arg max of L_i. (Notice that $T_2^* < T_1^*$ if the innovation is drastic. This is due to the traditional replacement effect). Let us first assume that $T_2 < T_1^*$. The solution to the adoption game is obtained by backward induction and is easy to guess. Imagine that no firm has adopted at date T_2^*. Then firm two would like to adopt since it will never be able to obtain a higher payoff. Knowing this firm one will want to adopt at $(T_2^* - \varepsilon)$ as $L_1(T_2^* - \varepsilon) > F_1(T_2^*)$; but then firm two will adopt at $(T_2^* - 2\varepsilon)$ as $L_2(T_2^* - 2\varepsilon) > F_2(T_2^* - \varepsilon)$, and so on. The outcome of the unique perfect equilibrium is that *firm one adopts at time* T_2. A correct formalization of the equilibrium strategies can be found in Fudenberg and Tirole [31][7].

---

7. Familiar strategies for continuous time games—called "distributional strategies"—are not "rich" enough to describe such preemption games. Richer and more satisfactory strategies are obtained by taking the limit of the continuous time model while allowing reasonable behavior.

Let us now check that $T_2 < T_1^*$ under the assumption that the current cost of adoption $f(t)$ decreases over time. T_1^* and T_2 are defined by:

$$(\pi_1^m - \pi_0^m) = rf(T_1^*) - f'(T_1^*)$$

and

$$\pi_2^d = rf(T_2).$$

Next notice that $\pi_2^d = (\bar{c} - c)D(c) > \displaystyle\int_c^{\bar{c}} D(p^m(\gamma))d\gamma.$

So $f(T_2) > f(T_1^*)$ or $T_2 < T_1^*$.

In the case of a drastic innovation, similar reasoning leads to the conclusion that adoption takes place at $T_1 = T_2$. The equilibrium then resembles the diffusion equilibrium in Fudenberg and Tirole [31]. Both firms have a positive probability of adopting first, but joint adoption never occurs.

The non-drastic outcome is highly reminiscent of the Gilbert-Newberry result. We obtain a persistence of monopoly, that is the incumbent adopts first.

This contrasts with the conventional wisdom, summarized in Scherer [84], that incumbents will tend not to adopt first, but will rather be "fast seconds". The difference is perhaps explained by Scherer's comment that "a monopolist... has little to gain by speeding up the introduction of product improvements *as long as others refrain from doing so...*" (emphasis added). In our model, as in Gilbert and Newberry, if the incumbent does not preempt the entrant will, because we are looking at *perfect* equilibria.

When competition in the product market is less extreme, the persistence of the monopoly result can be reversed. The simplest example is the following. Suppose as before that only the incumbent owns the old technology $\bar{c}$. Consider a "new" technology that is publicly available (at present cost $f(t)$), and that gives marginal cost $c = \bar{c}$. Clearly, the incumbent will never adopt this technology. The entrant however will adopt this technology as long as $\pi_2^d = \pi^d > 0$, and the current cost of adoption falls enough. So entry does occur, and furthermore, the "new" technology is adopted by the entrant "first".

The conclusions for the adoption model differ somewhat

from those for the R & D one. Before turning to some conjectures about why this is so, let us give an example of dynamic spatial competition that closely resembles the adoption game.

(c) Preemption in a spatial market

Here we give an elementary example that builds on the work of Prescott and Visscher [74] and especially Eaton and Lipsey [23]. Imagine a linear city of length one. To simplify the exposition assume that supermarkets can only be built at the two extremes of the city (this assumption is not crucial). At date 0, an incumbent serves the city with a supermarket located at the left end of the city. Consumers are uniformly distributed along the line, with density one. They have transportation cost t per unit of distance. At some future date T the population's density is expected to double (instantaneously). At any instant a supermarket can be built at constant cost f by either the incumbent or the entrant. Only the right end location is attractive to the entrant because of price competition and to the incumbent because it already has a supermarket on the left end. As long as no one has built a new supermarket the incumbent makes profit Π_0^m per unit of time ($2\Pi_0^m$ after T). If the incumbent builds first it makes profit $\Pi_1^m(>\Pi_0^m)$ per unit of time until T, and $2\Pi_1^m$ after T. If the entrant builds a supermarket first, each firm makes profit Π^d per unit of time before T and $2\Pi^d$ after T, with $2\Pi^d \leqslant \Pi_1^m$.[8] Note that we have implicitly assumed that if the entrant enters first at the right end of the city, the incumbent does not want to follow suit. Price competition there would drive the price down to marginal cost and would hurt even more the incumbent's left end supermarket. So there will be at most two supermarkets in the city.

With the same notation as for the adoption game $(L_i(t_1))(F_i(t_1))$ is firm i's intertemporal payoff when firm i invests first is

---

8. Assume that consumers have unit demands, that their surplus for the good sold by the firms is $\bar{s}$, and that a monopoly wants to cover the market (i.e., $\bar{s} \geqslant 2t$). If the firms have zero marginal cost then $\Pi_0^m = \bar{s} - t$, $\Pi_1^m = \left(\bar{s} - \dfrac{t}{2}\right)$, and $\Pi^d = t/2$. Hence, $2\Pi^d = t < \Pi_1^m$.

preempted) at the right end at time t_1): if $t_1 \leqslant T$:

$$\begin{cases} L_1(t_1) = \displaystyle\int_0^{t_1} \Pi_0^m e^{-rt}\mathrm{d}t + \int_{t_1}^T \Pi_1^m e^{-rt}\mathrm{d}t + \int_T^\infty 2\Pi_1^m e^{-rt}\mathrm{d}t - fe^{-rt_1} \\ F_2(t_1) = 0 \end{cases}$$

$$\begin{cases} L_2(t_1) = \displaystyle\int_{t_0}^{t_1} \Pi^d e^{-rt}\mathrm{d}t + \int_{t_1}^T 2\Pi^d e^{-rt}\mathrm{d}t - fe^{-rt_1} \\[2mm] F_1(t_1) = \displaystyle\int_0^{t_1} \Pi_0^m e^{-rt}\mathrm{d}t + \int_{t_1}^T \Pi^d e^{-rt}\mathrm{d}t + \int_T^\infty 2\Pi^d e^{-rt}\mathrm{d}t, \end{cases}$$

and similarly for $t_1 > T$.

We will assume that $\dfrac{2\Pi^d}{r} > f > \dfrac{\Pi^d}{r}$, i.e., that the entrant would want to invest at date T if it were the only firm able to invest. We will also assume that T is sufficiently large so that no firm will want to invest at time 0. L_i and F_i are pictured in figures:

Let T_1 and T_2 be defined by

$$L_1(T_1) = F_1(T_1) \text{ and } L_2(T_2) = F_2(T_2)$$

or

$$\int_{T_1}^T (\Pi_1^m - \Pi^d)e^{-rt}\mathrm{d}t + \int_T^\infty 2(\Pi_1^m - \Pi^d)e^{-rt}\mathrm{d}t = fe^{-rT_1}$$

and

$$\int_{T_2}^T \Pi^d e^{-rt}\mathrm{d}t + \int_T^\infty 2\Pi^d e^{-rt}\mathrm{d}t = fe^{-rT_2}.$$

Since $\Pi_1^m - \Pi^d > \Pi^d$, we have $T_1 < T_2$.

For exactly the same reason as for adoption under Bertrand competition in the unique perfect equilibrium, the incumbent will invest at the right end of the city at time $T_2 < T$. So there is persistence of monopoly. The analysis of pre-entry behavior (for example the choice of a cost level at the left end) is very similar to that for adoption (overinvestment to delay T_2).

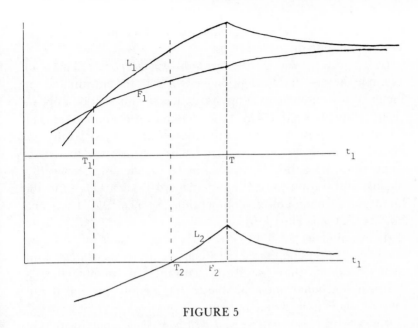

FIGURE 5

(d) The persistence of monopoly debate

The adoption and location models under Bertrand competition predict that monopolies will persist. As we, and Gilbert and Newberry
before us, explained, this is due to the fact that the incumbent has
more incentive to keep its monopoly than the entrant has to create
a duopoly. *In general, this efficiency effect is not sufficient for the persistence
of monopoly result.* It must also be the case that preemption be
"effective" and "deterministic". Preemption is effective if either a
patent physically prevents entry or price competition prevents a
second adopter from earning rents. If preemption is not effective, as
in the last example in the adoption game, the entrant may
preempt. A similarly more balanced conclusion is obtained when
preemption is non-deterministic, as in the R&D game. This is
because the date of preemption is random and because, by
investing more, the incumbent not only tends to preempt the
entrant, but also hastens its own replacement.

Even in a situation in which preemption is both effective and
deterministic, it is hard to believe that a monopoly *always* keeps its
privileged situation. We should therefore enrich the model so that

with some probability that monopolistic competition emerges. Let us mention four such extensions:

(i) *The monopoly may not have time to preempt the entrant*   This is for example the case in the adoption game if both the entrant and the incumbent would like to adopt as soon as the innovation appears ($F(0)$ relatively small). This lack of time to preempt can also be found in a disguised way in (static) models where there is only one period to invest; in this category let us mention the models of competition in location (d'Aspremont, Gabzewicz and Thisse [19], Shaked and Sutton [89], Champsaur and Rochet [17]) and the literature on monopolistic competition (Spence [91], Dixit and Stiglitz [22] and Hart [46]).

(ii) An obvious possibility is that *the incumbent does not possess the entrant's technology* and therefore can not duplicate its strategy a bit earlier. This is the case if the entrant can manufacture a differentiated good not available to the incumbent or if it can invest earlier than the incumbent.

(iii) A third reason can be *incomplete information*. Imagine that in the adoption or location games the incumbent is not quite sure about when the entrant wants to enter (for example the incumbent has a subjective distribution about the entrant's cost of entry). Then as the incumbent prefers to invest later than it is forced to by the need of preemption, it pays it to run a small risk of being preempted by the entrant (if for example the latter turns out to have a low entry cost). This is very similar to the exit game presented in section 6; there firms also make apparent mistakes due to incomplete information. This analogy is no coincidence as the exit game is a kind of reverse preemption game.

(iv) There can be *imperfect information*. The incumbent and the entrant may observe the adoption or location decision with a lag. If the entrant did not try to enter, the incumbent would delay its investment decision and it would pay the entrant to enter. And the entrant will try to enter only if it has some chance of being first, i.e., if there is some probability that monopoly won't persist. This model remains to be studied, and our guess is that information lags must be large for this phenomenon to be significant. An equilibrium of this kind is derived in Fudenberg, Gilbert, Stiglitz and Tirole [28] for an R&D game in which under perfect information only one firm does R&D while with information lags competition may arise.

Last we note that we have focused on the extreme case of an incumbent and an entrant. Does the persistence of monopoly under Bertrand competition still hold with two asymmetric firms initially in the market; that is, does the bigger one's market share tend to increase over time? Consider the case of a process innovation. With an incumbent and an entrant, we said that the incumbent gains more from deterring entry than the entrant from entering. More generally, does the bigger firm gain more from the innovation than the smaller one? The answer is not clear-cut. For static price competition, the bigger firm, which is the lower cost firm, drives its rival out of the market, so the situation resembles the incumbent/entrant model. In an auction, the bigger firm is willing to pay more than the smaller firm, so the efficiency effect is still valid. For quantity competition (or dynamic price competition), however, a new aspect may reverse the efficiency effect. We already know that monopoly need not persist under quantity competition, despite the efficiency effect. With two asymmetric firms engaged in quantity competition, the direction of the efficiency effect itself can be reversed, because the high-cost firm may then be producing a positive quantity. Thus from the viewpoint of productive efficiency, it may be desirable that the high-cost firm make the innovation rather than the low-cost firm. Leung [59] shows that this intuition may indeed hold for quantity competition. Kamien and Tauman [50] made an analogous remark when they noticed that an independent R&D firm may want to license its innovation to several firms when these compete through quantities.

4. SHORT-RUN COMMITMENT, FIXED COSTS, AND NATURAL MONOPOLIES

This section discusses two models of competition in natural monopolies, Eaton and Lipsey [24] and Maskin and Tirole [63]. In each model, the ability of the incumbent to make a short-run commitment to the market allows it to earn a profit despite the threat of entry. Moreover, in each model, the incumbent's equilibrium net present value goes to zero with the length of the commitment. Thus these models are consistent with the recent work of Grossman [43] and Baumol, Panzar, and Willig [6], who argue that incumbency gives a firm no advantage if commitments are impossible.

4a. Durability of capital

In the Eaton and Lipsey model, the product market is "blackboxed" to focus on capital as the state variable. In contrast to the capital *accumulation* literature, however, the capital stock has no influence on the flow profits. One unit of capital is simply a necessary cost of operation. A unit of capital has durability H and costs f. If only one firm is active its flow profit gross of capital costs is Π^m; if two firms operate each has flow profit Π^d, $\Pi^m > 2\Pi^d > 0$. The market is a natural monopoly, meaning that

$$\Pi^m \frac{(1 - \exp(-rH))}{r} > f > \Pi^d \frac{(1 - \exp(-rH))}{r}$$

so one firm could cover costs while two could not. The firms' sole decision variable is when to build a new unit of capital. One firm, the "incumbent," gets to choose first at time zero. As we will see, in equilibrium the incumbent rolls over its capital before it wears out in order to maintain its commitment to the market. If the incumbent replaces its capital every $(H - \Delta)$ years, then it is always committed to remain active at least Δ years after another firm enters, because Π^d is positive.

Eaton and Lipsey prove that there is a unique symmetric state-space equilibrium, in which the incumbent always replaces its capital Δ^* periods before it wears out, and the other firm never enters. Δ^* is the "optimal entry preventing policy," i.e. the minimum commitment to the market sufficient to deter entry. Let $V(\Delta^*)$ be the incumbent's value if it follows policy Δ^*; let $E(\Delta, \Delta^*)$ be the payoff to an entrant who builds a plant when the incumbent's commitment to the market is Δ, succeeds in driving the incumbent from the market and then adopts policy Δ^*. Then

$$E(\Delta, \Delta^*) = -f + \Pi^d \frac{(1 - \exp(-r\Delta))}{r}$$

$$+ \Pi^m \frac{(\exp(-r\Delta) - \exp(-r(H - \Delta^*)))}{r}$$

$$+ V(\Delta^*)\exp(-r(H - \Delta^*)). \tag{28}$$

A successful entrant pays capital cost f, shares the market until time Δ when the incumbent's capital expires, receives Π^m until $H - \Delta^*$, at which point it renews its plant. From this point the entrant's value is $V(\Delta^*)$. $E(\Delta, \Delta^*)$ can be rewritten more simply if we recognize that the difference between the payoff to successful entry and the incumbent's valuation is that the entrant receives Π^d from time 0 to Δ^*, while the incumbent receives Π^m. Thus

$$E(\Delta, \Delta^*) = V(\Delta^*) - (\Pi^m - \Pi^d) \frac{(1 - \exp(-r\Delta))}{r} \tag{29}$$

Because $E(\Delta, \Delta^*)$ is decreasing in Δ, the optimal entry-preventing policy satisfies

$$\Delta^* = \operatorname{argmax} V(\Delta), \text{ s.t. } E(\Delta, \Delta^*) \leqslant 0. \tag{30}$$

Both $V(\Delta)$ and $E(\Delta, \Delta^*)$ are decreasing in Δ, and so the maximization problem (30) is solved by finding a Δ^* such that $E(\Delta^*, \Delta^*) = 0$. Eaton-Lipsey show such a Δ^* exists and is unique by showing $E(\Delta, \Delta)$ is monotonically decreasing. Δ^* lies strictly between 0 and $H/2$. Moreover, no policy with a shorter commitment can deter entry. No $\Delta < \Delta^*$ can deter because for such Δ, $E(\Delta, \Delta^*) > 0 \sim \Delta > \Delta^*$ suffices to deter entry, but is overkill. Because $E(\Delta^*, \Delta^*) = 0$, from (29) we have

$$V(\Delta^*) = (\Pi^m - \Pi^d) \frac{(1 - \exp(-r\Delta^*))}{r} \tag{31}$$

Thus the threat of entry reduces the incumbent's value to the difference between the monopoly and duopoly profits for the length of the minimum commitment. As H and hence Δ^* go to zero, so does the incumbent's value. A final point, for completeness. The incumbent prefers playing Δ^* to allowing entry, because if entry occurs when the incumbent's capital will last Δ^* more period, the incumbent receives $\Pi^d(1 - \exp(-r\Delta^*))/r$, and $\Pi^m - \Pi^d > \Pi^d$.

We should point out that there are other equilibria in this model. For example, the outcome in which firms split the monopoly profit is a (non-state-space) equilibrium if H is sufficiently small: let the strategies be that firms alternate building plants every H years as long as such cooperation has been maintained so far; once someone deviates, both firms switch to the Eaton and Lipsey equilibrium. If H is sufficiently small the return to deviating is nearly zero and less than half the monopoly value. There also exist two asymmetric state-space equilibria that closely resemble those in Maskin and Tirole (to be described below).

Eaton and Lipsey go on to consider a model in which capital does not have a fixed life. Instead, firms must incur a stream of maintenance costs to prevent their capital from disintegrating. Under this assumption capital is not locked in when built. Once entry occurs we have at each instant a simultaneous move game as firms decide whether to continue maintenance. Thus it is not surprising that in this case there are several symmetric state-space equilibria. Eaton and Lipsey give an equilibrium for this case in which in the event of entry the incumbent exits once its maintenance expenditure exceeds Π^d. Eaton and Lipsey [24] were the first to consider the commitment value of finite-lived capital. Eaton and Lipsey [25] consider the same problem for the case of capital *accumulation* (as opposed to timing). They use an extension of the two-period models of Spence [92] and Dixit [20] to allow for depreciation. Before entry the incumbent invests up to some capacity level which it maintains until entry occurs. Eaton and Lipsey assume that upon entry the incumbent allows its capital stock to shrink to the "steady-state Cournot level" we introduced in the last section. Eaton and Lipsey motivate this assumption as a lower bound on the "aggressiveness' of the incumbent's response. Thus, they claim, if the incumbent could deter entry under the Eaton and Lipsey assumption it could do so in all equilibria. However, one plausible equilibrium in the post-entry game has its steady-state at the joint-profit-maximizing capital levels, which are below the Cournot point C. Such an "accommodating" post-entry equilibrium could provide more incentive to enter than the path going to C. We should stress that all of this is conjecture. The problem of finding *any* equilibrium for games of strategic investment with depreciation is yet unsolved. This is one of the two important problems in the strategic investment literature, the other being characterizing all the equilibria, a task left unsolved by Fudenberg and Tirole [30]. (A third and more general problem, that of a compelling method of choosing *between* equilibria, will need to await further developments in game theory.)

4b. Short-run commitment to production levels

Maskin and Tirole [63] provide a different model of short-run commitment in natural monopoly, which yields strikingly similar results. In (the simplest verion of) their model firms *alternate* choosing output (capacities) which are fixed for two periods. Firm one moves in odd periods and firm two in even ones, so in the obvious notation, $q^1_{2t+1} = q^1_{2t+2}$, and $q^2_{2t} = q^2_{2t+1}$. Choosing a nonzero output incurs fixed cost f for each of the two periods. The market is a natural monopoly, $2f > \Pi^m > f$. Firm i's flow profit in a period in which it produces is $\Pi^i(q_1, q_2) - f$; not producing yields a flow of zero. Firms maximize the expected net present value of profits, using common discount factor δ. The horizon is infinite.

In this model the state at time t is just the output level which was chosen in the previous period, so in the state-space formulation of the game, each firm's strategy is a "dynamic reaction function" specifying the output it will choose on its turn as a function of the most recent output choice of its opponent. Let $R_i(q)$ be firm i's "dynamic reaction function." (While Maskin and Tirole allow mixed strategies, there are no mixed-strategy equilibria in the model we will discuss.) If the Π^i_{12}, the cross-partial derivatives of firm i's flow profit are negative, the $R_i(q)$ will be nonincreasing, just as in the Cournot model.

Maskin and Tirole show that, if demand and costs are linear, there is a unique *symmetric* state-space equilibrium. If the discount factors are sufficiently near one (i.e., the periods are sufficiently short) this equilibrium has a particularly simple form:

Let q^* be the largest root of

$$\Pi(q, q) + \frac{\delta}{1-\delta} \Pi(q, 0) = \frac{f}{1-\delta}. \qquad (32)$$

If a monopolist maintains an output of q^* until entry occurs, the other firm is just indifferent between staying out of the market, and playing q^* itself forever, which incurs a loss of $\Pi(q^*, q^*) - f$ the first period, and a gain of $\Pi(q^*, 0) - f$ thereafter. Thus q^* corresponds to Δ^* (or $H - \Delta^*$) in Eaton and Lipsey—it is the optimal entry-deterring output level. $q > q^*$ overdeters entry, while $q < q^*$ fails to deter. This is the symmetric equilibrium if the discount factor is large enough that $q^* > q^m$, the monopoly output. When firms are patient, entry can be deterred but is not "blockaded." For smaller discount factors, the steady-state output is q^m. Since q^* satisfies (32), as δ tends to 1, $\Pi(q^*, 0)$ goes to f, so that instantaneous profit is driven down to the competitive level. Thus we again find that very short commitments confer little power.

This equilibrium is similar in spirit to the classic limit-pricing models of Bain and Sylos—by producing a larger output the incumbent sacrifices short-run profit to reduce the payoff to entry. The Bain and Sylos models have been criticized for the assumption that the incumbent's output is locked in once-and-for-all (or equivalently that the entrant *believes* it is). The Maskin and Tirole result demonstrates that limit-pricing can occur with short-run commitments: infinite-lived commitments are not necessary.

For sufficiently large fixed costs and discount factors there also exist two asymmetric equilibria in which one firm's reaction function is identically zero, and the other's is the best response to a rival who always (in every state) leaves the market. Given that firm one, say, believes firm two will always leave the market on its next move, then $R_1(q)$ solves

$$R_1(q) = \arg \max_{\tilde{q}} \left(\Pi(\tilde{q}, q) + \delta \Pi(\tilde{q}, 0) \right). \tag{33}$$

For any fixed cost $f < \Pi^m$, if the discount factor is sufficiently large, firm one will prefer playing according to (33) and then taking the market, to leaving it. Thus, the only way firm two can keep firm one out of the market is to choose output sufficiently large that the solution to (33) is zero. However, so large an output is unprofitable if the fixed costs are sufficiently large (greater than $9\Pi^m/14$). Thus firm two can do no better than to choose output zero, regardless of the current state. Along the equilibrium path, firm one deters entry by "refusing to believe" that firm two might choose nonzero output.

Let us point out that in Maskin and Tirole the state-space restriction is powerful. There is a continuum of perfect "supergame" equilibria in this model, but only three state-space equilibria. This contrasts sharply with the capacity-expansion model of Section 2, which had a continuum of state-space equilibria. Why the state-space restriction is much more powerful here is a topic for further research.

5. PRICE WARS AND TACIT COLLUSION

5a. The supergame approach

This section discusses two recent modifications of the supergame model of implicit collusion in oligopolies. Green and Porter [42] and Porter [72] assume that firms cannot directly observe the actions of their rivals, and that the market demand function is subject to random i.i.d. unobservable shocks. Because of the shock, firms can never be certain whether an unexpectedly bad outcome is due to some rival's "cheating." The noise thus reduces the extent to which the firms can collude. Brock and Scheinkman [12] study a price-setting supergame with capacity constraints. They assume that each firm has an exogenously given capacity, and conclude that the extent of collusion depends non-monotonically on the number of firms (or equivalently on the capital stock per firm). Collusion is difficult with a few firms, because total industry capacity provides an insufficient "threat", and is also difficult with many firms, because each firm's market share is too small, so that a firm has little to lose by undercutting. While we have been somewhat critical of the supergame approach, its simplicity allows these additional features to be added without making things intractable.

Let us sketch the Green and Porter model: there are n identical firms producing a homogeneous product. Firm i's output in period t is q_t^i; total output in period t is Q_t. Each period, firms set quantities, and the market price $\hat{p}_t$ is determined by

$$\hat{p}_t = p(Q_t)\theta_t, \tag{34}$$

where $p(\cdot)$ is the inverse demand function and θ_t is an i.i.d. disturbance not observed by the firms, with c.d.f. $F(\theta)$. That firms set outputs, not prices, is inessential, although it does make the assumption that firms do not observe their rivals' actions more plausible. Just as with the Matthews, Mirman and Saloner "smoothing" of the limit-pricing model (see Section 6), if the individual firms' choices are directly observable the noise becomes irrelevant. Porter also treats the case of additive, rather than multiplicative noise, although the solution is harder to characterize.

Let $\Pi^i(q^1, \ldots, q^n)$ be firm i's (expected) single-period profit function and let $q_c = (q_c^1, \ldots, q_c^n)$ be a Cournot equilibrium. (Porter's results are for linear demand and uncertainty and for convex c.d.f.'s F). Now restrict attention to the following set of "trigger-price" equilibria. Fix a "collusive" output $q^* \equiv Q^*/n$, a trigger price $\tilde{p}$, and a punishment length T. Initially firms play q^*, and continue to do so until the first time the observed price is less than $\tilde{p}$. Once this occurs, switch to the Cournot equilibrium q_c for T periods, and then revert to the collusive output q^*. At least one trigger-price equilibrium exists because we can take $q^* = q_c$. If all firms are playing such trigger price strategies, the probability of a punishment phase is Prob $(\tilde{p} > \theta p(Q^*)) = F(\tilde{p}/p(Q^*)) \equiv \alpha^*$. Each firm's payoff is then

$$V^i(q^*, \ldots, q^*) = \frac{\Pi^i(q_c)}{1-\delta} + \frac{\Pi^i(q^*) - \Pi^i(q_c)}{1 - \delta + (\delta - \delta^T)\alpha^*} \tag{35}$$

where δ is the firms' discount factor. Thus the expected value equals the value if firms produced at the Cournot output, plus a term representing the expected discounted value of cooperation. Note that if $\alpha^* = 0$, $V^i(q^*) = \Pi^i(q^*)/(1-\delta)$. For $\{q^*, \tilde{p}, T\}$ to be an equilibrium, it is necessary and sufficient that no firm wish to change its output in the collusive phase (no firm will deviate in the punishment phase because q_c is a Cournot equilibrium). The first-order conditions for no firm to deviate are particularly simple in the case $T = \infty$ (i.e., unrelenting punishment),

$$\frac{\partial \Pi^i}{\partial q^i}(q^*) = \delta \frac{\partial}{\partial q^i}[\text{Prob}(p < \tilde{p})] \cdot \frac{[\Pi^i(q^*) - \Pi^i(q_c)]}{1 - \delta + \delta\alpha^*} \tag{36}$$

so that the marginal gains to cheating are just balanced by the (discounted) costs of triggering punishment.

The *optimal* cartel policy maximizes each firm's expected value over $(q^*, \tilde{p}, T)$ given the constraint that firms shouldn't want to deviate from q^*. Porter solves that maximization, and shows that while the optimal punishment length T may be finite or infinite, in either case the optimal quantity $q^* = \hat{q}$ strictly exceeds the joint-profit-maximizing level q_m but that $\hat{q}$ converges to q_m as the variance of the noise goes to zero. $\hat{q}$ strictly exceeds q_m because at q_m increasing each firm's output has no first-order effect on profits in the collusive phase, but decreases the incentive to cheat (the right-hand side of (36) if $T = \infty$), which permits a lower trigger-price $\tilde{p}$ and fewer "price wars." It is not surprising that $\hat{q} \to q_m$ as the noise vanishes, because $\tilde{p}$ can then be made very near to the expected price if none cheated. What is more surprising is the likelihood that the best attainable valuation is not continuous in the discount factor for a given noise. As firms become more patient collusion becomes easier, just as in repeated games with observable actions. If firms are totally patient, then as Radner [75] has shown, they can enforce the first-best even with nonnegligible noise by using strategies which cause the probability of punishment to converge to zero over time. This requires nonconstant trigger prices. (A recent example of Radner, Myerson and Masking [76] suggests the possibility that even the limit of the best outcome enforceable by any equilibrium need not be the first best—that is the set of enforceable payoffs may be discontinuous in the discount factor when actions are not observable. Fudenberg and Maskin [29] show the enforceable set *is* continuous in the discount factor at $\delta = 1$ with observable actions. The best attainable payoff with constant trigger prices is (presumably) continuous as the discount factor goes to one, but whether this limit is the "first-best" is less clear.)

Green and Porter and Porter offer three related motivations for their work. First, their model was inspired by Stigler's (non-game-theoretic) treatment of secret price cutting in oligopoly. As in Stigler, firms cannot observe each others' actions but must infer them from the behavior of the market. Second, in the standard supergame models of efficient collusion punishment is never observed, while in these trigger-price papers punishment occurs with positive probability. Finally, their model can be viewed as a test of the robustness of supergame analysis to a small and reasonable perturbation. Porter's results suggest that at least in his special linear case the supergame analysis is robust to the addition of a small amount of "moral hazard". As we noted above, the small-noise case is probably the most relevant, because firms often have fairly good information about the prices of their competitors. The problem with small noise is that price wars are correspondingly infrequent. (One sidelight on Stigler: in his model, firms indeed competed on prices, not quantities. Firms did not observe their rivals' prices but inferred them from their own shares.)

The trigger price models do yield periodic "price wars," but as Green and Porter acknowledge, the observed price wars aren't really "punishments," because no firm ever defects from the cartel (i.e., the collusive strategies). Quoting Green and Porter, "the market price ... never leads (firm) i's competitors to revise their beliefs about how much i has produced." Stigler's theory that firms occasionally defect and are punished entails that such revision of beliefs occurs, and thus requires that private information exists. Green and Porter believe, however, that private information is of secondary importance in many industries. To model tacit collusion in oligopolies in which private information *is* important one would use the Bayesian-equilibrium approach of the next section. If in each period each firm's cost or demand function received an idiosyncratic shock which was private information, one would expect there to be equilibria in which firms usually "cooperated," but it was understood that firms would deviate (and be punished!) when conditions were particularly favorable. In such a model the optimal equilibria would probably have positive probabilities of punishment.

A final motivation for the Green and Porter paper was to develop a theoretical basis for an empirical study of oligopolies. In particular the Green and Porter model can be estimated and tested on time-series data for a single industry. Such data and tests avoid many of the problems of interpretation that plague cross-section empirical studies. The reader may have noticed that this is the first mention of econometric analyses in these notes. Green and Porter may be the first authors since Stigler to develop the econometric implications of a dynamic model of oligopoly (see also the work of e.g., Bresnahan [11] which, while at the industry level, is based on static models). The growing complexity of theoretical models of oligopoly, coupled with a reaction again the "reduced-form" cross-section regressions of the sixties and early seventies, has convinced many practitioners that the oligopoly problem is too complex for econometric analysis and that only reliable source of empirical information is the "case study." While such descriptive studies are indeed a rich source and important source, we believe (hope) that Green and Porter may be a signal of things to come. As the techniques of dynamic models diffuse throughout the profession, econometric analyses of dynamic oligopoly may become more common. We should add that Porter has in fact applied the Green and Porter model to the U.S. railroad industry of the nineteenth century.

One small criticism of the econometric part of Green and Porter: their model has a heavy time-series structure. In particular, price wars are always preceded by unusually low demand. Green and Porter's econometric implementation of their model ignores this time-series structure. Instead they use a static "switching regressions" simultaneous equations model to (independently) assign each observation to either the "collusive" or "punishment" regime and then estimate the cost and demand equations. If their theoretical model is correct their empirical model will have correlated errors and lagged endogenous variables. Furthermore, the only tests implemented by Porter [73] were against the alternatives of Cournot and purely collusive behavior. The more flexible switching-regressions model performs better, but this only tells us that markups weren't constant, something we knew before the analysis.

Brock and Scheinkman [12] offer a model of price competition under capacity constraints. There are n firms producing a homogenous good, each with exogenously given capacity K. They have identical marginal cost of production c. The Walrasian (notional) demand is $D(\min_i p_i)$. Consider first the static simultaneous-move price game. As is well-known from Edgeworth, this game may or may not have a pure strategy equilibrium. If K is small, the equilibrium price is such that the demand is nK. If K is big, the equilibrium price is c. If K is intermediate, the equilibrium must involve mixed strategies. Let $\Pi^N(K, n)$ denote the resulting individual profit for any value of K. It can be checked that Π^N decreases with n.

Now consider the repeated game version. Firms play a price $\hat{p}$ (such that $D(\hat{p}) \leqslant nK$) until some firm deviates. In the latter case the firms play the static Nash equilibrium described above, forever. The cost to deviating is $\dfrac{\delta}{1-\delta}\left[\dfrac{D(\hat{p})}{n}(\hat{p} - c) - \Pi^N(K, n)\right]$, where δ denotes the discount factor. In order for $\hat{p}$ to be a sustainable price it must be the case that the immediate gain from deviating does not exceed this loss. The short-run gain to deviating is the increase in market share. By charging a price just under $\hat{p}$, a firm is able to sell up to its capacity. The short-run gain is then $(\hat{p} - c)\left(K - \dfrac{D(\hat{p})}{n}\right)$. $\hat{p}$ must thus satisfy:

$$\frac{\delta}{1-\delta}\left[\frac{D(\hat{p})}{n}(\hat{p} - c) - \Pi^N(K, n)\right] \geqslant (\hat{p} - c)\left(K - \frac{D(\hat{p})}{n}\right)$$

or

$$\frac{D(\tilde{p})}{n}(\hat{p} - c) \geqslant \delta\Pi^N(K, n) + (1 - \delta)K(\hat{p} - c). \qquad (37)$$

Brock and Scheinkman use a linear demand version of this model, compute $\Pi^N(K, n)$ and derive the optimal $\hat{p}$ for the firms under the constraint (37).

Like Green and Porter, Brock and Scheinkman pick the best symmetric outcome associated with a simple class of trigger strategies. They are therefore able to derive some comparative statics for profits and prices as functions of n and K.

An interesting result in Brock and Scheinkman is that increasing the number of firms has a nonmonotonic effect on $\hat{p}$. Consider equation (37). Increasing n decreases a given firm's market share for a given $\hat{p}$, $(D(\hat{p})/n)$. Therefore it increases the firm's incentive to undercut and sell K units. This makes $\hat{p}$ more difficult to sustain. On the other hand, changing n changes the threat point.

A bigger n means a lower Π^N. Therefore the firms have less incentive to deviate from $\hat{p}$. In that sense a large aggregate capacity helps firms to collude by making defection very costly. Brock and Scheinkman indeed show that the highest cartel profit per firm is obtained for an intermediate number of firms.

As the authors observe, the chief limitation of their analysis is that the choice of capacity is exogenous. One would not expect K to remain fixed as the number of firms changes.

Making K endogenous is no easy task. First mixed strategy equilibria (or at least their payoffs) have to be computed for any vector of capacity choices. Even with simple rationing schemes this requires complicated derivations (see Kreps and Scheinkman [53]). This is a computational problem, but not a fundamental difficulty. More serious is the issue of the dynamic price equilibrium under asymmetric capacities. Incentives for price deviation differ among firms. It becomes impossible to appeal to the optimal symmetric equilibrium consistent with trigger strategies. The lack of focal equilibrium throws us back into the morass of supergame equilibria.

It is not yet clear what the effect of an endogenous choice of capacities would be. Choosing a high capacity increases the strength of the punishment; but it makes it harder to sustain high prices because of the bigger temptation of a price cut. It seems plausible that, as Brock and Scheinkman conjecture, endogenizing the capacity choice will lead to excess capacity, as in the example in Maskin and Tirole [64].

5b. Short-run commitments

The Green and Porter and the Brock and Scheinkman approaches to price collusion are attempts to obtain positive results from the supergame paradigm. They restrict punishment to be of the simple trigger kind and they pick the best equilibrium consistent with this type of punishment. If the level of noise in Green and Porter is small, or if capacities in Brock and Scheinkman are big, the monopoly price is sustainable for high discount factors. As in usual in the supergame literature, firms punish their opponents (or themselves!) not because they are currently hurt by their opponents' past moves, but simply because they expect their competitors to do the same. This is the familiar bootstrap aspect of supergame equilibria.

If one wants to develop a theory in which firms react only to actions that currently affect them (i.e., a state-space theory), one immediately faces the familiar Bertrand enigma: In a simultaneous move price equilibrium with identical firms and constant marginal cost, firms sell at the competitive price and make zero profit. This outcome, which also holds for the finitely repeated game, is counterintuitive for at least two reasons. First, one would not expect pure competition with a small number of firms. Second, casual observation suggests that a firm does react when the other firms' price badly affects its current profit. But the very concept of "real reaction" is automatically ruled out if past choices do not influence current payoffs.

Maskin and Tirole [64] offer a theory of dynamic price competition that formalizes the idea of reaction. More precisely it exploits the dual notions of reaction and commitment. In order for a firm to react to its opponent's action it must be the case that the latter's action is fixed at least in the very short run; otherwise the opponent will have changed its action in the meantime and the firm will not react to anything. Short-run commitments are the key to reaction. In the context of price competition one may, for example, imagine that changing price "all the time" is costly, so that the firms set prices that are valid for some period of time exceeding the basic decision period.

The first step in the Maskin and Tirole analysis is to study the consequences of a model in which firms are forced to react to each other. The second step is to check that the presumed timing is indeed the equilibrium timing when firms are free to move when they wish subject to the constraint that their move implies a short-run commitment of fixed length. In this section we simply discuss the first stage of the analysis by way of an example. The endogenization of the timing, although crucial, is of a more technical nature and won't be analyzed here.

Consider a duopoly producing perfectly substitutable goods. Demand is linear: $D(p_1, p_2) = 1 - \min(p_1, p_2)$. Production costs are zero and capacities are unlimited. Firms can charge prices $p_i = i/6$ where $i = 0, 1, \ldots, 6$. Firms take turns choosing prices:

Firm one (two) chooses in odd (even) periods. Once firm one chooses $p_{1,t}$, it is committed to this price for two periods: $p_{1,t+1} = p_{1,t}$; and similarly for firm two. Both firms maximize the present discounted value of their profits $\sum_{t=0}^{\infty} \delta^t \Pi^i(p_{i,t}, p_{j,t})$.

As before a Markov (or state space) perfect equilibrium is a perfect equilibrium in which firms use "payoff-relevant strategies." What is the payoff relevant state? Imagine that firm one plays. Firm two is still committed to its past price p_2. Therefore this price currently affects firm one's profit and hence belongs to the state. Maskin-Tirole posit that firm one's reaction is a function of the state only, $p_1 = R_1(p_2)$, and similarly for firm two. Now consider the following symmetric strategies: $R_1 = R_2 = R$.

Π	p	$R(p)$
0	p_6	p_3
5	p_5	p_3
8	p_4	p_3
9	p_3	p_3
8	p_2	p_1
5	p_1	$\begin{cases} p_3 \\ p_1 \end{cases}$ (mixed strategy)
0	p_0	p_3

where the Π column indicates the aggregate profit when the lowest price is p (multiplied by 36; $p_3 = \frac{1}{2}$ is the monopoly price). These strategies form a Markov perfect equilibrium for sufficiently high discount factors (in price competition one would expect commitments to be short and therefore the relevant discount factor to be close to one). The interpretation of this equilibrium closely resembles the classic kinked-demand curve story. There is a focal price, here the monopoly price. If a firm raises its price above the focal price, the other firm does not follow suit. However, if a firm prices under the focal price, it gains market share, makes short-run gains but triggers a price war. Hurting the other firm, it forces the latter to react. It turns out that the long-run costs of the price war outweigh the short-run gain for the aggressive firm.

In this equilibrium, price wars are not observed in the long run. There also exists another type of equilibrium price dynamics, called Edgeworth cycles, in which price wars are continuously observed except for short periods of relenting.

Maskin and Tirole characterize the set of equilibria for discount factors close to one, and more general price grids and profit functions. The main conclusions are:

1. The monopoly price and prices nearby are sustainable as focal prices.

2. In any symmetric equilibrium the average aggregate profit is at least half the monopoly profit.

The latter conclusion as well as the economic story underlying the behavior differ substantially from those associated with the supergame paradigm.

As we said, the above is only the first step in the Maskin and Tirole analysis. They also show that firms will in fact choose to alternate price changes if both firms are free ex ante to move in any period (but prices are still locked in for two periods). This provides some support for the timing they analyzed. Of course, ideally one would prefer that the interval between price changes was not fixed, but firms chose to change prices only "occasionally" because of costs of adjustment. A fixed life time for commitments is more plausible for capital (as in Eaton and Lipsey) than for price. This idea is pursued in Anderson [1] in a supergame context.

A last point: this theory immediately suggests a theory of excess capacity. Imagine that in the equilibrium depicted above each firm accumulated only a capacity equal to the steady state output 1/4. Then the threat to wage a price war if the other undercuts is not credible anymore. A firm would not be able to supply the market at a price lower than p_3. An example in Maskin and Tirole shows that firms may want to choose a capacity considerably higher than the one that is used on the equilibrium path. This example is unfortunately very simplistic, with firms choosing between two capacities at the start and then playing the price game. One could envision firms continuously choosing capacities and prices, with the capacity changes being much slower than price changes. The lesson of this simplistic example is, as in Brock and Scheinkman, that large capacities may allow firms to maintain price collusion.

Finally we should observe that the state-space restriction still allows many equilibria in this model. Given this multiplicity the conclusion that arbitrarily short commitment bound the equilibrium profit away from zero is quite strong.

6. INVESTING IN DISINFORMATION

6a. Introduction

History matters not only through its effect on tangible variables, but also through the information it conveys to competitors. Oligopolists are concerned by many variables they cannot estimate precisely. Among these are the cost structure or more generally the objective function of their opponents, the state of the market or its potential, etc. Competitors may also have trouble observing each others' actions. Oligopolistic interaction must then be formalized as a situation of incomplete or imperfect information. In such a world actors may want to

1. exploit the lack of information of their opponents;
2. manipulate the latter's information in order to derive benefits later on.

This second aspect explains the phrase "investment in disinformation." Although information is not a tangible variable, beliefs at a given date belong to the state of the system; and to the extent that they can be influenced before that date, they give rise to a certain kind of investment. Moreover, just as with tangible variables, the history of the competition can be summarized by state variables. Formal models of investment in disinformation had to await the development of dynamic games of incomplete information, which combine the perfectness idea (Selten [87]) with the theory of games of incomplete information, (Harsanyi [45]). This gives rise to the concept of perfect Bayesian or sequential equilibrium (for a formal presentation of these techniques, see Kreps and Wilson [55]). Briefly, a perfect Bayesian equilibrium of a dynamic game of incomplete information is a set of history-dependent strategies and beliefs (where the beliefs specify the players' subjective probabilities at each state of the game) satisfying for any history:

(P) The strategies are optimal given the beliefs.

(B) The beliefs are Bayes-consistent with the strategies and the observed actions.

The sequential equilibrium concept places slightly more consistency restrictions on the beliefs than (B). (B) places no restrictions on what players believe after observing an action which in equilibrium has zero probability.

We distinguish three branches of the strategic signalling literature:

(i) Firms send signals that are aimed at deterring entry. This is the case in Milgrom and Roberts' [67] incomplete-information version of the limit-pricing story. There the incumbent may want to choose a low price to induce the entrant to believe either that demand is low or that the incumbent has a low cost. In the Kreps and Wilson [55]—Milgrom and Roberts [68] resolution of the chain-store paradox, an incumbent may want to fight an entrant to have other potential entrants be confused as to whether the incumbent might not indeed enjoy fighting. If the entrant believes with some positive probability that the incumbent may be "irrational," then such a policy may be successful.

(ii) Firms send signals that are aimed at inducing more cooperative market behavior from their rivals. We refer to Kreps, Milgrom, Roberts and Wilson's [52] work on the repeated prisoner's dilemma. The starting point of their analysis is that there may be some probability that the other firms have a simple (nonoptimal) strategy like "cooperate unless others have cheated, retaliate otherwise," and that a rational firm would want the others to believe that it is "irrational" in order to discipline them.

(iii) Firms send signals that are aimed at inducing exit. Here we allude to our own work on the transposition of the war of attrition to oligopolies. (Fudenberg and Tirole [33].) The basic idea is that, when selection is necessary (i.e., some firms must exit), it may take a while to occur because of informational asymmetries. Since each firm would like to be the one that remains, either time or financial constraints or both settle the issue. The signals that are sent in such games include the length of time that the firms remain active and possibly the prices. It should also be noted that war-of-attrition type games can also be applied to repeated games involving entry (Kreps and Wilson [56]).

Clearly all these models have much in common. So will have the numerous other applications that will follow the pioneering work of Kreps, Milgrom, Roberts and Wilson. A remark is in order: Incomplete information does not necessarily lead to an aggressive outcome. The Kreps, Milgrom, Roberts and Wilson [52] approach to market discipline implies that in equilibrium firms do not hurt each other (except at the end of the horizon).

After this somewhat lengthy introduction, let us discuss the research program initiated by these papers. We will focus on the formalism and the techniques using the examples of limit-pricing and the war of attrition. We will in particular examine the issues of multiplicity of equilibria and of their robustness to the information structure. And we will conclude with some personal opinions about the use of dynamic games of incomplete information for the study of dynamic oligopoly.

6b. Limit-pricing and entry deterrence

The idea underlying limit-pricing (Bain [4]) is the following A monopoly may be able to deter entry by conveying signals to the potential entrants that entry is not profitable. Assume, as Milgrom and Roberts [67], Matthews and Mirman [65] and Saloner [80] do, that there is one potential entrant and that this entrant has incomplete information about the incumbent's cost. If the incumbent played its static monopoly price naively, i.e., as if there were no threat of entry, the entrant could easily infer the incumbent's cost. But this cannot be an equilibrium situation. The incumbent would want to reduce its price in order to fool the entrant. But a rational entrant will perceive the possibility of such a strategy. In turn, the incumbent knows that the entrant won't be so easily fooled. And so on, and so forth. The perfect Bayesian equilibrium concept precisely formalizes this infinite regress.

A simplified model   Let us give a simplified version of Milgrom and Roberts' [67] model that contains many of the relevant features. There are two periods. In the first, firm one is a monopoly and chooses a price p_1. Firm two is a potential entrant. It observes p_1 and decides whether to be in the market in the second period or not. All the relevant market parameters (costs, demands) are common knowledge but firm one's unit cost c_1. c_1 can take two values $\underline{c}_1 < \bar{c}_1$, each with probability $1/2$. Firm two's profit, net of entry cost, is $\Pi_2^d(\underline{c}_1)$ or $\Pi_2^d(\bar{c}_1)$, and zero if it does not enter. Notice that we omitted the common knowledge variables in the definition of Π_2^d. Also, we implicitly assume that the entrant, if it does enter, immediately knows the incumbent's cost (we'll come back to this assumption later on). To have a nontrivial problem, assume that

$$\Pi_2^d(\underline{c}_1) < 0 < \Pi_2^d(\bar{c}_1),$$

i.e., if the entrant has complete information, it would enter only if the incumbent has a high cost. Assume further that without any market information, the entrant would want to enter. Assuming risk neutrality, this implies that:

$$\frac{1}{2}\left(\Pi_2^d(\underline{c}_1) + \Pi_2^d(\bar{c}_1)\right) > 0.$$

Last, let $\bar{\Pi}_1(p_1)(\underline{\Pi}_1(p_1))$ denote the high cost (low cost) incumbent's first period strictly quasi-concave profit function; and let $\delta\bar{\Pi}_1^m$ and $\delta\bar{\Pi}_1^d(\delta\underline{\Pi}_1^m$ and $\delta\underline{\Pi}_1^d)$ denote the high cost (low cost) incumbent's discounted second period profit when it is in a situation of monopoly or duopoly. Obviously

$$\bar{\Pi}_1^m > \bar{\Pi}_1^d \text{ and } \underline{\Pi}_1^m > \underline{\Pi}_1^d.$$

Imagine that firm one behaves naively, i.e., ignores the threat of entry. It chooses the monopoly price in the first period: $\underline{p}_1^m$ or $\bar{p}_1^m$ $(\underline{p}_1^m < \bar{p}_1^m)$. The entrant then observes the incumbent's cost and enters when $p_1 = \bar{p}_1^m$. Again, in order not to have a trivial solution, we will assume that the high cost monopoly would want to fool the entrant in such a situation:

$$\bar{\Pi}_1^m - \bar{\Pi}_1(\underline{p}_1^m) < \delta(\bar{\Pi}_1^m - \bar{\Pi}_1^d).^9$$

Now consider rational firms. The monopoly chooses a first period price that depends on its costs: $p_1(c_1)$. The entrant observes p_1,[10] and forms beliefs about c_1. Let $\underline{q}(p_1)$ $(\bar{q}(p_1) = 1 - \underline{q}(p_1))$ be the posterior probability that the incumbent has a low (high) cost. We require $\underline{q}(\cdot)$ to be Bayes-consistent with the monopolist's strategy $p_1(\cdot)$. The entrant then compares $\{\underline{q}(p_1)\Pi_2^d(\underline{c}_1) + \bar{q}(p_1)\Pi_2^d(\bar{c}_1)\}$ and zero to decide whether to enter or not. Thus the incumbent can infer an entry decision as a function of p_1. We then require $p_1\{\cdot\}$ to be intertemporally optimal for the incumbent given its costs and the entrant's reaction to p_1.

A priori there can be several regimes:

(a) Pooling: the monopoly's price does not depend on c_1.

(b) Separating: different types of monopoly charge different prices.

(c) Semi-separating: the two types separate or pool in a random manner (using mixed strategies).

To solve for a perfect Bayesian equilibrium we consider a particular regime, compute the entrant's belief associated with this regime and the entrant's associated optimal strategy, and check that the different types of monopolist indeed want to behave consistently with the presupposed regime.

(a) First, assume that the equilibrium is pooling. The entrant's posterior after observing the equilibrium price p_1 satisfies $\underline{q}(p_1) = 1/2$. And from our assumption the entrant enters. But each type would then prefer (strictly prefer for at least one type) playing its first period monopoly price: it cannot make less first

---

9. This assumption is not necessary with a continuum of costs for both the entrant and the incumbent. By lowering p_1 a bit under the monopoly price, the incumbent loses only second-order first-period profit and deters some entry under naive expectations.

10. By a slight abuse of notation we use the same letters for actions and strategies. The distinction is easily made by noticing that strategies are functions (or correspondences).

period profit and it cannot deter less entry. Thus there cannot exist a pooling equilibrium.

(b) Second, assume that the equilibrium is separating. Let $\underline{p}_1$ and $\bar{p}_1$ denote the low and high cost incumbent's first period equilibrium price. The entrant enters (stays out) when observing $\bar{p}_1(\underline{p}_1)$. Let's start by noticing that $\bar{p}_1 = \bar{p}_1^m$: $\bar{p}_1^m$ maximizes the high cost incumbent's first period profit and can not induce more entry than $\bar{p}_1$ does. Let us now derive necessary conditions for $\underline{p}_1$. It must be the case that the high cost incumbent does not want to fool the entrant by charging $\underline{p}_1$:

$$\bar{\Pi}_1^m - \bar{\Pi}_1(\underline{p}_1) \geqslant \delta(\bar{\Pi}_1^m - \bar{\Pi}_1^d) \tag{38}$$

It must also be the case that the low-cost firm does not lose too much money to separate in the first period. In particular the low cost incumbent could play its monopoly price, and would at worst encourage entry. That this cannot be optimal is formalized by:

$$\underline{\Pi}_1^m - \underline{\Pi}_1(\underline{p}_1) \leqslant \delta(\underline{\Pi}_1^m - \underline{\Pi}_1^d) \tag{39}$$

To go further one has to make additional assumptions on the second-period duopoly outcomes. Since such a development is not our purpose here, we content ourselves with noting that one can find reasonable conditions on second-period competition so that (38) and (39) amount to

$$p' \leqslant \underline{p}_1 \leqslant p''(< p_1^m)$$

where p' and p'' satisfy (38) and (39) with equality.

Conversely, assume that $\underline{p}_1$ satisfies (38) and (39). Are $\bar{p}_1$ and $\underline{p}_1$ equilibrium actions? To answer this question, we must specify what happens when the monopoly deviates from its presumed equilibrium strategy. Assume that $p_1 \neq \underline{p}_1, \bar{p}_1$ is played. Since this price has a zero probability in equilibrium, we can specify any beliefs we want for the entrant. For the monopoly not to deviate from the equilibrium strategy, it must in particular be the case that even if the entrant has beliefs $q(p_1) = 0$, and therefore enters, the monopolist does not want to play p_1. Specify $q(p_1) = 0$. Then from (39) and $\underline{\Pi}_1(p_1) \leqslant \underline{\Pi}_1^m$, type $\underline{c}_1$ does not want to play p_1. And since $\bar{\Pi}_1(p_1) \leqslant \bar{\Pi}_1^m$, type $\bar{c}_1$ does not want to play p_1 either. Thus by specifying $q(p_1) = 0$ for all $p_1 \neq \underline{p}_1, \bar{p}_1$, we have obtained an equilibrium.

Thus it is easy to derive a continuum of equilibria indexed by $\underline{p}_1$. Note that in these equilibria, the low-cost firm limit-prices, but entry is not affected.

(c) We also leave it to the reader to check that there also may exist lots of semi-separating equilibria.

Multiplicity The limit-pricing game exhibits an unfortunate multiplicity of equilibria. This "excessive" multiplicity comes from the fact that beliefs are not pinned down by Bayes rules out of equilibrium and can be chosen to induce certain behaviors (compare below another type of multiplicity that can arise in a war of attrition). This works as follows: some prices can be ruled out as equilibrium outcomes by specifying beliefs that are very optimistic for the entrant. For such prices the entrant enters, and a posteriori we have been justified to rule out these prices as being desirable (equilibrium) prices for the incumbent. This problem is particularly acute in our example in which there are only two types of incumbent and a continuum of first period potential prices. But this problem also pops up in Milgrom and Roberts [67] who assume a continuum of types for the incumbent (although with a continuum of types there is only one equilibrium in which first-period price is strictly decreasing in the incumbent's cost).

As we have seen, this type of multiplicity arises from the leeway one has in forming out-of-equilibrium conjectures. A natural trick to eliminate this type of multiplicity is to ensure that most, if not all, possible actions are equilibrium actions in order for Bayes rule to pin beliefs down. This is precisely what is done in Matthews and Mirman [65] and Saloner [80]. Let us examine how this works. Consider the previous model. Following Matthews, Mirman and Saloner, assume that the incumbent chooses a quantity q_1, and that the corresponding market price is a random function of this quantity: p_1 has a density $f(p_1|q_1)$ on $(0, +\infty)$. The entrant observes p_1 only (we'll come back to this assumption later on). Assume that the price "stochastically decreases" with the quantity, i.e., $(f(p_1|q_1))/(f(p'_1|q_1))$ decreases with q_1 if $p_1 > p'_1$. Next, following Saloner, make the monotonicity assumption that lower-cost firms choose higher quantities; this is the case in the noiseless separating equilibria described above (this assumption, while reasonable, ought to be the object of a separate study). The entrant's optimal strategy is then to enter if and only if the observed price exceeds some entry deterring price $\bar{p}$. The incumbent's objective function is then

$$\Pi_1(q_1, c_1) + \delta(\text{Prob}(p_1 \geqslant \bar{p}|q_1)\Pi_1^d(c_1) + \text{Prob}(p_1 < \bar{p}|q_1)\Pi_1^m(c_1))$$

where $\Pi_1(q_1, c_1)$ denotes its expected first-period profit given q_1 and c_1. The optimal strategy is then a function of $\bar{p}$ and c_1. We then see that $\bar{p}$ is a fixed point solution of the following problem: let $\underline{q}_1(\bar{p})$ and $\bar{q}_1(\bar{p})$ denote the optimal quantities for the two types given $\bar{p}$, and let $p^d(q_1, \bar{q}_1)$ denote the entry deterring level given the equilibrium actions $\underline{q}_1$ and $\bar{q}_1$. Then

$$\bar{p} = p^d(\underline{q}_1(\bar{p}), \bar{q}_1(\bar{p})).$$

Saloner shows that one indeed gets a unique equilibrium (satisfying the monotonicity condition).

General remarks about this method of solving the multiplicity problem are in order.

First, it seems to us that testing the robustness of equilibria to small amounts of noise in the system is basically sound. Perfect and complete information about some variables can only be expected to be an approximation. And we saw that the knife-edge aspect of perfect information introduces lots of equilibria by forbidding Bayes rule to have any grip on beliefs following certain actions. Therefore we fully agree with Matthews, Mirman and Saloner that robustness of equilibria to the information structure is a desirable property. This attitude actually follows the spirit of the use of games of imperfect and incomplete information.

Second, we have some trouble interpreting the particular form of noise that is chosen by Mirman, Matthews and Saloner. The incumbent chooses a quantity and lets the market determine the price. It is not clear what institution implements this. This problem is important because the effectiveness of noise in singling out one equilibrium depends crucially on the form of noise. Imagine, for example, that the incumbent chooses the prices and faces an uncertain demand; then we are back to the Milgrom and Roberts formulation. The entrant observes a price that is an ungarbled function of the incumbent's cost. Introducing noise is then pointless in that it amounts to replacing the incumbent's first period profit by an expectation. Next, imagine that the price is chosen after a demand shock which is not known to the entrant. The price is then a function of the incumbent's cost and the demand shock. Still some prices may be ruled out by "optimistic beliefs." Adding a quantity (i.e., capacity) choice before the demand shock (in the style of Kreps and Scheinkman) would not alter this problem—that the market price, which is usually observed by the entrant, is chosen by the incumbent. Maybe one way to escape this problem is to assume that 1) the incumbent sells through retailers, 2) the retailer's current cost and 3) the price contract between the incumbent and the retailers are unknown to the entrant. Even so, it is not clear that beliefs can always be pinned down by Bayes rule.

Milgrom and Roberts (unpublished notes) use another method to select among equilibria. This method is very similar to the iterated elimination of dominated strategies (see, e.g., Moulin [70]). The particular application to the limit-pricing problem goes as follows. Beliefs for an out-of-equilibrium price p_1 which is "dominated" for the higher cost firm (but not for the low-cost firm) are constrained to put all the weight on the low-cost firm. By domination we mean that the high cost firm is better off playing its equilibrium price rather than p_1 *whatever the entrant's beliefs at p_1*. This is a bit like putting a zero-probability of tremble on dominated strategies.

Now it is easy to see that such constraints on beliefs get rid of most equilibria: If $p_1 \leqslant p''$, playing p_1 is dominated by playing $\bar{p}_1^m$ for the high cost entrant. Therefore $\underline{q}(p_1) = 1$ and the entrant does not enter when it observes p_1. Then the only remaining separating equilibrium is $(\bar{p}_1^m, p'')$, where the low cost firm plays the highest price that allows it to differentiate from the high cost firm. There also exist semi-separating equilibria in which the low cost firm plays p'' and the high-cost firm randomizes between $\bar{p}_1^m$ and p'' (as long as the probability of playing p'' is not too high). This multiplicity is irrelevant in that in all these equilibria the entrant enters (does not enter) when observing $\bar{p}_1^m(p'')$. And the payoffs of the two types of incumbent are the same. So there is no problem of coordination among equilibria.

We feel that this way of selecting among equilibria is very natural. More rigorously, this selection can be justified by the Kohlberg and Mertens [51] concept of strategic stability, which is a refinement of perfect Bayesian equilibrium.

Policy Implications   The Milgrom and Roberts analysis was very helpful in destroying certain myths; for example, that limit pricing is always successful in deterring entry and is detrimental to welfare. On the other hand, few conclusions seem to emerge. According to Kreps-Spence: "The one unambiguous result is that, as long as the entrant is less likely to enter the higher the pre-entry quantity and the lower the pre-entry price, the monopolist will always provide more than or at least just as much as the pre-entry profit maximizing quantity." Actually, it is not even clear that the entrant is always less likely to enter the lower the pre-entry price. As we noticed earlier an important assumption in this limit-pricing literature is that the entrant knows the incumbent's cost immediately after entry. It is easy to show that in a price game (with differentiated products, say), a firm would like the other firm to believe that it has *higher* costs than it really has. This is because, typically, 1) reaction curves are upward sloping in static price games, and 2) a firm's price increases with its own cost. Thus in an incomplete information situation the entrant will play less aggressively if it believes the incumbent has a high cost. Now, this may in some cases reverse the limit-pricing conclusion (take a situation in which, because of low entry costs, entry is not really an issue). The incumbent may thus charge a high first period price to signal high costs.[11] Of course, we believe the traditional limit-pricing story to be more plausible, but this illustrates how few general conclusions can be derived in this context. Also a number of extensions of the basic model are desirable. Saloner [80] has done some progress on the multi-period problem. The robustness to multiple incumbents is also an issue. With two or more firms in the market, deterring entry becomes a public good

---

11. This was independently observed by Bulow, Geankoplos and Klemperer [13].

from the point of view of these firms (see, e.g., Bernheim [8], Gilbert and Vives [40]).

6c.   Wars of attrition and selection

We now give an example of "bilateral predation." Imagine that there are n operating (or potential) firms in a market that is viable for only $m < n$ firms. This may, for example, be the case of industries whose technology involves a fixed cost of production. This may also be the case for R&D competition under static or dynamic (learning by doing) returns to scale. Selection must then operate in order for the firms not to lose money. Conventional theory tells us little about how the remaining firms are picked and why selection is not immediate (i.e., why there exists periods of time over which firms lose money but do not leave the market).

Theoretical biologists have analyzed this kind of situation. For example, animals may spend time or energy in a seemingly useless fight for a prey (see, e.g., Maynard Smith [66] and Bishop, Cannings and Maynard Smith [10]). Economists have recently been interested in the game theoretic aspects of this kind of fight and in its analogy with a second-bid auction (Riley [79], Milgrom and Weber [69]). It is clearly tempting to apply the war of attrition concept to models of economic conflicts that are not resolved instantaneously (market selection, strikes, etc.). An unfortunate feature of the model of animal war is that typically there exist lots of equilibria (a continuum of them in Riley [79]). This fact may seriously compromise the predictive power of such a theory. In this section we discuss the multiplicity problem. We notice that its nature differs somewhat from the multiplicity encountered in the limit-pricing model, and we explain why all equilibria but one are not robust to small and plausible perturbations in the information structure. The model we use is a stripped down version of Fudenberg and Tirole [33].

Consider a duopoly operating under increasing returns. The two firms have incomplete information about their rival's fixed costs.[12] Let Π_i denote firm i's instantaneous duopoly profit (net of

---

12. We rule out incomplete information about the rival's variable cost in order to be able to avoid instantaneous signalling through prices and focus on the war of attrition. Again we blackbox the product market.

fixed cost). Π_i is known to firm i, but not to firm j, for whom Π_i is distributed on $[-\infty, 0]$ according to the continuous density g. Note that we are implicitly assuming that there is a natural monopoly. Let $V^m(\Pi)$ denote the present discounted value of being a monopolist for a firm that has instantaneous duopoly profit Π. Clearly $dV^m/d\Pi > 0$. Let $\underline{\Pi} < 0$ be such that $V^m(\underline{\Pi}) = 0$. Assume for simplicity that the game starts at time zero and that reentry is not allowed. The model can be enriched somewhat, for instance by allowing learning and asymmetric payoffs (see Fudenberg and Tirole [33]).

Let us now exhibit two perfect Bayesian equilibria of this game: Equilibrium number one: If both firms are still in the market at time t, firm two drops out and firm one stays, whatever their profit levels. The firms' beliefs about their rival is still given by g (truncated at $\underline{\Pi}$). Equilibrium number two: switch the firms' names.

It is clear that this type of behavior is rational given the rival's behavior. In equilibrium number one, firm one is extremely "macho." Its behavior amounts to saying, "I'll stay in no matter what." Firm two has then to yield. In equilibrium number two the roles are switched. These equilibria actually are not the only ones, since Riley [79] has shown that, for a related war of attrition, there can be a continuum of equilibria.[13] These equilibria are intermediate between the two polar ones exhibited here, and can be indexed by a degree of "relative machoness."

We would like to explain why equilibrium behavior is not easily pinned down for this information structure. Let us give a very informal and incomplete resolution of this problem (for details, see Fudenberg and Tirole [33]). Let $\Phi_i(t)$ denote firm i's profit if, at time t, firm i is indifferent between staying in and dropping out. It is easy to see that Φ_i must be nondecreasing. This results from the self-selection constraints of the game: A firm is willing to stay longer, the lowest its current loss. It can also be shown that Φ_i is

---

13. The difference between Riley's approach and ours is that in the animal war there is no correlation between fighting costs and the reward. This game corresponds to $V^m(\Pi) = V^m > 0$ for all Π; and hence $\underline{\Pi} = -\infty$. This changes the condition at $t = 0$ somewhat, but not in a substantial way as we will see below.

continuous and (except at time zero) differentiable. Next $\Phi_i(0)$ must equal $\underline{\Pi}$: A firm with duopoly profit under $\underline{\Pi}$ loses money as a duopoly and does not want to become a monopoly. Firms with profits strictly exceeding $\underline{\Pi}$ do not want to drop out immediately because there is a strictly positive probability that their opponent drops out at the start. Let us now derive the differential equations for (Φ_1, Φ_2). Between t and $(t + \mathrm{d}t)$, firm i, if it has duopoly profit $\Phi_i(t)$, loses $(-\Phi_i(t)\mathrm{d}t)$. On the other hand, with probability $[\Phi_j'(t)[(g(\Phi_j(t))/(1 - G(\Phi_j(t))))\mathrm{d}t]$, firm j drops out. $(g(\cdot)/(1 - G(\Phi_j(t))))$ is the conditional probability distribution given that firm j has not quit by time t. Thus for firm i with duopoly profit $\Phi_i(t)$ to be indifferent between staying and quitting:

$$\Phi_i(t) + V^m(\Phi_i(t))\left(\Phi_j'(t)\frac{g(\Phi_j(t))}{1 - G(\Phi_j(t))}\right) = 0. \qquad (40)$$

Thus we obtain a pair of differential equations in (Φ_1, Φ_2). Is the solution pinned down by the two boundary conditions $\Phi_1(0) = \Phi_2(0) = \underline{\Pi}$? The answer is no. The RHS of the differential equations are not Lipschitz at $t = 0$; $V^m(\Phi_i(0)) = 0$ implies that $\Phi_j'(0)$ is "infinite". This fact reintroduces some leeway in the solution. Roughly speaking, the "relative slope" of Φ_1 and Φ_2 at $t = 0$ is not determined, so that the boundary conditions do not really pin down the solution. And indeed one can obtain lots of equilibria.

A crucial assumption on the subjective distribution is that it stops at 0. Imagine that it does not, so that $G(0) < 1$. In other words there is a strictly positive (but possibly small) probability that the player "enjoys fighting." For animal wars, this can be due to some machoness or suicidal instinct. Another interpretation can be supplied for economic wars. The possibility that a firm makes money as a duopoly (or loses money on this market, but gains overall because of spillover effects) is hard to rule out with certainty.

Clearly a firm with strictly positive duopoly profit never drops out (staying in is a dominant strategy). Let us now show that the two equilibria exhibited above aren't equilibria any more. Take equilibrium number one for instance. Firm one, if it observes that firm two is still in at time $t \geqslant 0$, ought to infer that firm two has a positive duopoly profit, and therefore will not drop out. Then firm one, if it has a negative duopoly profit, ought to leave. This equilibrium therefore is not robust to small perturbations in the information structure.

What about other potential equilibria? In Fudenberg and Tirole [33], we show that there actually exists a unique equilibrium. The argument is somewhat involved, but a crucial step in the proof consists in noticing that in equation (40), $(1 - G(\Phi_j(t)))$ does not converge to zero when t goes to infinity (whereas it does when $G(0) = 1$). When $G(0) = 1$, $\lim_{t \to \infty} \Phi_j(t) = 0$. If the limit were strictly negative, some firms would have $(-\infty)$ with strictly positive probability! This allows us to "pin things down at infinity" and to rule out multiplicity.

If learning is introduced, the way multiplicity is ruled out is more explicit: Imagine that learning is "high enough" so that a firm that is intertemporally viable as a monopoly eventually becomes intertemporally viable as a duopoly (if this is not the case, we are back to the previous treatment). Then in the long run, there won't be selection anymore. Now it is easy to see that a firm with a negative duopoly profit does not stay in the market if, with conditional probability one, the other stays in forever. Therefore both firms must "stop dropping out" at the same time T. And moreover at this time T, the intertemporal duopoly profit from T on must be equal to zero for $\Phi_i(T)$ (i.e., for the type that is indifferent between dropping out and staying in). In other words, we have added a new (and somewhat unconventional) boundary condition; and this boundary condition singles out a unique equilibrium (which is the symmetric one here).

DISCUSSION

We pointed out that zero-probability events created problems by not allowing Bayes rule to pin beliefs down. This problem, if it exists for the two equilibria exhibited in 2), does not arise for the intermediate Riley type equilibria in the animal war of attrition. In these equilibria (see Riley [79]), there is at each instant a strictly positive probability that each player stays until that instant. Hence the variety of equilibria has nothing to do with out-of-equilibrium conjectures, but more with some (vague) notion of "degree of machoness."

We want to point out the (equally vague, but we hope interesting) analogy between this type of multiplicity, and a more familiar type of multiplicity. Consider the traditional static Nash bargaining problem of dividing a pie of size 1 between two players. And assume that these two players make simultaneous demands (d_1, d_2) as to the share they want. If $d_1 + d_2 \leqslant 1$, the demands are satisfied; if $d_1 + d_2 > 1$, players get nothing. It is well known that for this game, there exists a continuum of pure strategy equilibria: Any pair $(d_1^*, 1 - d_1^*)$ for $d_1^* \in [0, 1]$ is in equilibrium. As in the animal war of attrition, these equilibria are somehow indexed by the "relative power" of the two players. Each would like to convince the other that it will demand a high share.

Nash [71] and Binmore [9] succeeded in picking a unique equilibrium precisely by introducing a small uncertainty as to the size of the pie and by taking the limit as the uncertainty disappears, namely Nash's [71] bargaining solution $(1/2, 1/2)$. In our work on the war of attrition, we also solve the multiplicity problem by perturbating beliefs (i.e., by introducing a small probability that the market is not a natural monopoly).

Beyond the methodological relationship, there is also an economic analogy. Both problems in a sense deal with a division of a pie. Therefore they both have an aspect of a public good. There is a conflict between the "public" interest (selection; sharing the cake) and the private interest (resisting longer than one's rival; obtaining a big share). In both games it turns out that small uncertainty imposes a cost on "excessive greed," and rules out a "diversity of power relationships."

This subsection used continuous-time models with incomplete information. Continuous-time models are very convenient for studying games of timing or of lumpy decisions, but they may create three (related) problems. First, strategies are functionals rather than simple functions. Second, the infinite number of periods may give rise to supergame phenomena (as noticed in

Kreps and Wilson [56]). Third, in the context of games of incomplete information, too much information may be conveyed by an action. An action at a single time has no effect on payoffs (only an interval of actions does), but can have a nonnegligible effect on beliefs. This seems a bit paradoxical. More work is required to understand the structure of such games.

6d. Conclusions

We would like to conclude with some personal opinions about the use of dynamic games of incomplete information. These thoughts clearly are time- and knowledge-dependent.

A criticism that, over the last years, has been addressed to this approach is that one can explain "anything" with incomplete information (see Fudenberg and Maskin [29] for a formal demonstration). Thus in a formal sense, games of incomplete information would not have much more predictive power than super-games. However, it may be easier to decide which small perturbations of the game are reasonable than to choose between the supergame equilibria directly. We may often have a good idea of what types of incomplete information are likely. Whether or not one believes in Milgrom and Roberts' version of limit-pricing depends on whether one thinks that incomplete information about the incumbent's cost or demand has empirically significant effects.

Another criticism often addressed to the incomplete information approach is that even for a given information structure, there may still be a lot of equilibria. We have discussed this at length and we believe that the problem is not hopeless. We argued in favor of checking which equilibria are robust to small and plausible changes in the information structure. Indeed, even without the problem of selecting among equilibria, this procedure would still be desirable in view of the uncertainty we face as to which information structure is relevant and whether this information structure is really common knowledge.

As we have observed, outcomes of games may be very sensitive to the information structure. Some would take this to be an argument against games of incomplete information, but this remark is also a criticism of (solutions of) games of perfect information that are not robust to small and plausible perturbations in the information structure. Let us give two examples of this phenomenon. First Kreps, Milgrom, Roberts and Wilson in several papers have shown that important reputation effects can be built on very little uncertainty about the opponents' payoffs. Second, in our work on the adoption of a new technology (the discrete-time model Fudenberg and Tirole [32]), we showed that introducing a small uncertainty about the rival's motivation or competence may change a unique equilibrium into a more plausible and equally unique equilibrium that differs radically. In both cases, a tiny bit of incomplete information breaks too rigorous a backwards induction. Since we believe that the perfectness idea has considerable power, we think it is sound to rule out absurd perfect equilibria on the basis of informational considerations rather than by rejecting the equilibrium concept. Again in view of the uncertainty we face in determining the information structure of practical games, we plead in favor of robustness to its specification.

The upshot of all this is that economists have given themselves a powerful and dangerous tool, namely, dynamic games of incomplete or imperfect information. Its dangers ought to induce us to check the robustness of our conclusions, because information is usually imperfect.

REFERENCES

1. Anderson, R. "Quick-Response Equilibria," mimeo, 1983.
*2. Arrow, K. "Economic Welfare and the Allocation of Resources to Innovation," in *The Rate and Direction of Economic Activity*, ed. by R. Nelson. Cambridge, Mass.: National Bureau of Economic Research, 1962.
3. Aumann, R. "Mixed and Behavior Strategies of Infinite Extensive Games," in *Annals of Mathematics Studies*, **52** (1964), 627–650. Princeton, N.J.: Princeton University Press.
4. Bain, J.: "A Note on Pricing in Monopoly and Oligopoly," *American Economic Review*, **39** (1949), 448–464.
5. Baldani, J.: "Strategic Advertising and Credible Entry Deterrence Policies," mimeo, 1983.
6. Baumol, P., J. Panzar, and R. Willig: *Contestable Markets and the Theory of Industry Structure*. New York: Harcourt Brace Jovanovich, 1982.
7. Benoit, J. P.: "Entry with Financial Constraints," mimeo, 1983.
8. Bernheim, D.: "Strategic Deterrence of Sequential Entry into an Industry," mimeo, 1982.
9. Binmore, K. C.: "Nash Bargaining, II," mimeo, 1981.

10. Bishop, D., C. Cannings, and J. Maynard Smith: "The War of Attrition with Random Rewards," *Journal of Theoretical Biology*, **74** (1978), 377–388.
11. Bresnahan, T.: "Competition and Collusion in the American Automobile Industry: The 1955 Price War," mimeo, 1980.
*12. Brock, W., and J. Scheinkman: "Price Competition in Capacity-Constrained Supergames," mimeo, 1980.
13. Bulow, J., J. Geanakoplos, and P. Klemperer: "Multimarket Oligopoly," mimeo, 1983.
14. Butters, G.: "Equilibrium Distributions of Sales and Advertising Prices," *Review of Economic Studies*, **44** (1977), 465–491.
*15. Caves, R., and M. Porter: "From Entry Barriers to Mobility Barriers," *Quarterly Journal of Economics*, **9** (1971), 241–267.
16. Chamberlain, E.: "Duopoly: Value Where Sellers are Few," *Quarterly Journal of Economics*, **40** (1929), 63–100.
17. Champsaur, P., and J. C. Rochet: "Product Differentiation and Duopoly," mimeo, 1984.
18. Dasgupta, P., and J. Stiglitz: "Uncertainty, Industrial Structure, and the Speed of R&D," *Bell Journal of Economics*, **11** (1980), 1–28.
19. d'Aspremont, C., J. Gabzewicz, and J. F. Thisse: "On Hotelling's Stability in Competition," *Econometrica*, **47** (1979), 1145–1150.
*20. Dixit, A.: "A Model of Duopoly Suggesting a Theory of Entry Barriers," *Bell Journal of Economics*, **10** (1979), 20–32.
21. Dixit, A.: "The Role of Investment in Entry Deterrence," *Economic Journal*, **90** (1980), 95–106.
22. Dixit, A., and J. Stiglitz: "Monopolistic Competition and Optimum Product Diversity," *Review of Economic Studies*, **43** (1977), 217–235.
23. Eaton, B. C., and R. G. Lipsey: "The Theory of Market Preemption: The Persistence of Excess Capacity and Monopoly in Growing Spatial Markets," *Economica*, **46** (1979), 149–158.
*24. Eaton, B. C., and R. G. Lipsey: "Exit Barriers are Entry Barriers: The Durability of Capital as a Barrier to Entry," *Bell Journal of Economics*, **11** (1980), 721–729.
25. Eaton, B. C., and R. C. Lipsey: "Capital, Commitment, and Entry Equilibrium," *Bell Journal of Economics*, **12** (1981), 593–604.
26. Encaoua, D., P. Geroski, and A. Jacquemin: "Strategic Competition and the Persistence of Dominant Firms: A Survey," in *New Developments in the Analysis of Market Structure*, ed. by F. Mathewson and J. Stiglitz. Boston, Mass.: MIT Press, 1984.
27. Friedman, J.: *Oligopoly and the Theory of Games*. Amsterdam: North-Holland, 1977.
28. Fudenberg, D., R. Gilbert, J. Stiglitz, and J. Tirole: "Preemption, Leap-frogging, and Competition in Patent Races," *European Economic Review*, **22** (1983), 3–31.
*29. Fudenberg, D., and E. Maskin: "Folk Theorems for Repeated Games with Discounting and with Incomplete Information," mimeo, 1983.
*30. Fudenberg, D., and J. Tirole: "Capital as a Commitment: Strategic Investment to Deter Mobility," *Journal of Economic Theory*, **31** (1983a), 227–256.

31. Fudenberg, D. and J. Tirole: "Learning by Doing and Market Performance," *Bell Journal of Economics*, **14** (1983b), 522–530.

*32. Fudenberg, D., and J. Tirole: "Preemption and Rent Equalization in the Adoption of New Technology," mimeo, 1983c, forthcoming *Review of Economic Studies*.

33. Fudenberg, D., and J. Tirole: "A Theory of Exit in Oligopoly, mimeo, 1983d.

34. Fudenberg, D., and J. Tirole: "Predation without Reputation," mimeo 1984.

35. Gaskins, D. W.: "Dynamic Limit Pricing: Optimal Pricing under Threat of Entry," *Journal of Economic Theory*, **3** (1971), 306–322.

36. Gelman, J., and S. Salop: "Judo Economics," mimeo, 1982.

37. Geroski, P., and A. Jacquemin: "Dominant Firms and their Alleged Decline," *International Journal of Industrial Organization*, **2** (1984).

38. Gilbert, R., and R. Harris: "Competition and Mergers with Lumpy Investment," mimeo, 1982.

*39. Gilbert, R., and D. Newberry: "Preemptive Patenting and the Persistence of Monopoly," *American Economic Review*, **72** (1982), 514–526.

40. Gilbert, R., and X. Vives: "Non-Cooperative Deterrence of Sequential Entry," mimeo, 1983.

*41. Green, E., and R. Porter: "Noncooperative Collusion under Imperfect Price Information," *Econometrica*, **52** (1984), 975–994.

42. Grossman, G., and C. Shapiro: "Informative Advertising with Differentiated Goods," *Review of Economic Studies*, **51** (1984), 63–82.

43. Grossman, S.: "Nash Equilibrium and the Industrial Organization of Markets with Large Fixed Costs," *Econometrica*, **49** (1981), 1149–1172.

44. Harris, C., and J. Vickers: "Perfect Equilibrium in a Model of a Race," mimeo, 1983.

*45. Harsanyi, J.: "Games of Incomplete Information Played by Bayesian Players," *Management Science*, **14** (1967), 159–182, 320–334, 486–502.

46. Hart, O.: "Monopolistic Competition in the Spirit of Chamberlin," ICERD D.P., London School of Economics, 1983.

47. Jacquemin, A.: "Stratégies d'Enterprise, Structures de Marché, et Contrôle Optimal," *Revue d'Economie Politique*, **82** (1972), 1104–1118.

48. Jørgensen, S.: "A Survey of Some Differential Games in Advertising," *Journal of Economic Dynamics and Control*, **4** (1982), 341–369.

49. Judd, K.: "Credible Spatial Preemption," MEDS D.P. 577, Northwestern University, 1983.

50. Kamien, M., and Y. Tauman: "The Private Value of a Patent: A Game Theoretic Analysis," mimeo, 1983.

*51. Kohlberg, E., and J. F. Mertens: "Strategic Stability of Equilibria," Harvard Business School, mimeo, 1984.

*52. Kreps, D., P. Milgrom, J. Roberts, and R. Wilson: "Rational Cooperation in the Finitely Repeated Prisoners' Dilemma," *Journal of Economic Theory*, **27** (1982), 245–252.

*53. Kreps, D., and J. Scheinkman: "Quantity Precommitment and Bertrand Competition Yield Cournot Outcomes," *Bell Journal of Economics*, **14** (1983), 326–338.

*54. Kreps, D., and A. M. Spence: "Modelling the Role of History in Industrial

Organization and Competition," in *Contemporary Issues in Modern Microeconomics*, ed. by George Feiwel. London: McMillan, 1984.

55. Kreps, D., and R. Wilson: "Reputation and Imperfect Information," *Journal of Economic Theory*, **27** (1982a), 253–279.

56. Kreps, D., and R. Wilson: "Sequential Equilibria," *Econometrica*, **50** (1982b), 863–894.

57. Lee, T., and L. Wilde: "Market Structure and Innovation: A Reformulation," *Quarterly Journal of Economics*, **94** (1980), 429–436.

58. Lesourne, J.: *Modèles de Croissance des Entreprises*. Paris: Dunod, 1973.

59. Leung, H.-M.: "Preemptive Patenting: The Case of Co-Existing Duopolists," mimeo, 1984.

60. Levine, J., and J. Thépot: "Open Loop and Closed Loop Equilibria in a Dynamical Duopoly," W.P. 81–36, E.I.A.S.M., Brussels, 1981.

61. Lieberman, M.: "The Learning Curve, Pricing, and Market Structure in the Chemical Processing Industries," Ph.D. thesis, Harvard University, 1982.

62. Loury, G.: "Market Structure and Innovation," *Quarterly Journal of Economics*, 93 (1979), 395–410.

*63. Maskin, E., and J. Tirole: "A Theory of Dynamic Oligopoly, I: Overview and Quantity Competition with Large Fixed Costs," mimeo, 1982.

*64. Maskin, E., and J. Tirole: "A Theory of Dynamic Oligopoly, II: Price Competition," mimeo, 1984.

65. Matthews, S., and L. Mirman: "Equilibrium Limit Pricing: The Effects of Private Information and Stochastic Demand," *Econometrica*, **51** (1983), 981–996.

66. Maynard Smith, J.: "The Theory of Games and the Evolution of Animal Conflicts," *Journal of Theoretical Biology*, **47** (1974), 209–221.

*67. Milgrom, P., and J. Roberts: "Limit Pricing and Entry under Incomplete Information," *Econometrica*, **50** (1982a), 443–460.

*68. Milgrom, P., and J. Roberts: "Predation, Reputation and Entry Deterrence," *Journal of Economic Theory*, **27** (1982b), 280–312.

69. Milgrom, P., and R. Weber: "Distributional Strategies for Games with Incomplete Information," *Mathematics of Operations Research*, 1984.

70. Moulin, H.: "Dominance-Solvable Voting Schemes," *Econometrica*, **47** (1979), 1337–1351.

71. Nash, J.: "The Bargaining Problem," *Econometrica*, **18** (1950), 155–167.

72. Porter, M.: *Competitive Strategy*. New York: The Free Press, 1980.

73. Porter, R.: "Optimal Cartel Trigger Price Strategies," *Journal of Economic Theory*, 29 (1983), 313–338.

74. Prescott, E., and M. Visscher: "Sequential Location among Firms with Foresight," *Bell Journal of Economics*, **8** (1977), 378–394.

75. Radner, R.: "Optimal Equilibria in Some Repeated Games with Imperfect Monitoring," mimeo, 1981.

76. Radner, R., R. Myerson, and E. Maskin: "An Example of a Repeated Partnership Game with Discounting and with Uniformly Inefficient Equilibrium," mimeo, 1983.

77. Reinganum, J.: "Dynamic Games of Innovation," *Journal of Economic Theory*, **25** (1981), 21–46.

*78. Reinganum, J.: "Uncertain Innovation and the Persistence of Monopoly," *American Economic Review*, **73** (1983), 741–748.

79. Riley, J.: "Strong Evolutionary Equilibrium and the War of Attrition," *Journal of Theoretical Biology*, **83** (1980), 383–402.
80. Saloner, G.: "Dynamic Equilibrium Limit Pricing in an Uncertain Environment," mimeo, 1981.
81. Salop, S. E., ed.: *Strategy, Predation and Antitrust Analysis.* Washington, D.C.: Federal Trade Commission, 1981.
82. Schelling, T. C.: *The Strategy of Conflict.* Cambridge, Mass.: Harvard University Press, 1960.
83. Scherer, F.: "Research and Development Resource Allocation under Rivalry," *Quarterly Journal of Economics*, **81** (1967), 359–394.
84. Scherer, F.: *Industrial Market Structure and Economic Performance*, 2nd edition. Chicago: Rand McNally College Publishing Company.
85. Schmalensee, R.: "Product Differentiation Advantages of Pioneering Brands," *American Economic Review*, **72** (1982), 349–365.
86. Schmalensee, R.: "Advertising and Entry Deterrence: An Exploratory Model," *Journal of Political Economy*, **90** (1983), 636–653.
87. Selten, R.: "Spieltheoretische Behandlung eines Oligopolmodells mit Nachfrageträgheit," *Zeitschrift für die gesamte Staatswissenschaft*, **12** (1965), 301–324.
88. Selten, R.: "The Chain-Store Paradox," *Theory and Decision*, **9** (1978), 127–159.
89. Shaked, A., and J. Sutton: "Natural Oligopolies," *Econometrica*, **51** (1983), 1469–1483.
90. Simaan, M., and T. Takayama: "Game Theory Applied to Dynamic Duopoly Problems with Production Constraints," *Automatica*, **14** (1978), 161–166.
91. Spence, A. M.: "Product Selection, Fixed Costs, and Monopolistic Competition," *Review of Economic Studies*, **43** (1976), 217–235.
92. Spence, A. M.: "Entry, Capacity, Investment and Oligopolistic Pricing," *Bell Journal of Economics*, **8** (1977), 534–544.
93. Spence, A. M.: "Investment Strategy and Growth in a New Market," *Bell Journal of Economics*, **10** (1979), 1–19.
*94. Spence, A. M.: "The Learning Curve and Competition," *Bell Journal of Economics*, **12** (1981), 49–70.
95. Starr, R., and Y. C. Ho: "Nonzero-Sum Differential Games," *Journal of Optimization Theory and Applications*, **3** (1967a), 184–206.
96. Starr, R., and Y. C. Ho: "Further Properties of Nonzero-Sum Games," *Journal of Optimization Theory and Applications*, **4** (1967b), 207–219.
97. Stigler, G.: "A Theory of Oligopoly," *Journal of Political Economy*, **72** (1964), 44–61.
98. Telser, L.: "Cutthroat Competition and the Long Purse," *Journal of Law and Economics*, **9** (1966), 259–277.
99. Von Weizsäcker, C. C.: *Barriers to Entry: A Theoretical Treatment.* Berlin: Springer-Verlag, 1980.
100. Wilson, R.: "Reputation in Games and Markets," mimeo, 1983.

In keeping with the format of this series, we have marked the references most closely related to our monograph with an asterisk. This designation is not intended to indicate the relative merits of the papers.

INDEX